HMH Georgia Science

This Write-In Book belongs to

_____

Teacher/Room

_____

Houghton Mifflin Harcourt™

Printed in the U.S.A.

ISBN 978-1-328-86861-9

9 10 0868 26 25 24 23

4500867304   B C D E F G

Consulting Authors

Michael A. DiSpezio
Global Educator
North Falmouth, Massachusetts

Marjorie Frank
*Science Writer and Content-Area Reading
    Specialist*
Brooklyn, New York

Michael Heithaus
Dean, College of Arts and Sciences
Florida International University
North Miami, Florida

Georgia Reviewers

C. Alex Alvarez, Ed.D
Director of STEM and Curriculum
Valdosta City Schools
Valdosta, Georgia

Kristen N. Brooks
2nd Grade Teacher
Lindsey Elementary School
Warner Robins, Georgia

Melissa Davis
K–5 Science Coordinator
Atlanta Public Schools
Atlanta, Georgia

Natasha Luster-Knighton
5th Grade Science Teacher
Radium Springs Elementary
Albany, Georgia

Amy Materne
Russell Elementary School
Warner Robins, Georgia

Erin Neal
2nd Grade Teacher
White Oak Elementary School
Newnan, Georgia

Mark Christian Rheault
K–5 Specialist
Union County Elementary
Blairsville, Georgia

Kolenda Thomas-McDavis
5th Grade Science Ambassador
Northside Elementary
Warner Robins, Georgia

Christina Voigt
Teacher
Lake Joy Elementary
Warner Robins, Georgia

Dora A. Waite
Georgia State Science Ambassador
Russell Elementary
Warner Robins, Georgia

Contents

Track Your Progress

EARTH AND SPACE SCIENCE

PHYSICAL SCIENCE

LIFE SCIENCE

Investigating Questions

Big Idea

Scientists raise questions about Earth and the universe and seek answers to some of them by careful investigation.

Naples, Florida

I Wonder Why

Scientists work on the beach as well as many other places. How do scientists help animals survive? *Turn the page to find out.*

Here's Why Scientists get their hands dirty! They use tools such as tags, cameras, notes, and maps to help animals survive.

In this unit, you will explore the Big Idea, the Essential Questions, and the Investigations on the Inquiry Flipchart.

Levels of Inquiry Key ■ DIRECTED ■ **GUIDED** ■ INDEPENDENT

Track Your Progress

Big Idea Scientists raise questions about Earth and the universe and seek answers to some of them by careful investigation.

Essential Questions

Now I Get the Big Idea!

Science Notebook

Before you begin each lesson, be sure to write your thoughts about the Essential Question.

Essential Question

How Do Scientists Investigate Questions?

Engage Your Brain!

Find the answer to the following question in this lesson and record it here.

How is this student acting like a scientist?

_____

_____

_____

Active Reading

Lesson Vocabulary

List each term. As you learn about each, make notes in the Interactive Glossary.

_____ _____

_____ _____

_____ _____

_____

Use Headings

Active readers preview, or read, the headings first. Headings give the reader an idea of what the reading is about. Reading with a purpose helps active readers understand what they are reading.

What Is Science?

Science is about Earth and everything beyond it. What does a scientist look like? To find out, take a look in the mirror!

Active Reading As you read these two pages, underline the main idea.

Why do volcanoes erupt?

Look for a Question

How does a butterfly use its six legs? What does the shape of a cloud tell about the weather? It's never too soon to start asking questions! Write your own question below.

_____

_____

Science is a way of looking at the world and thinking about it. When you think like a scientist, you ask questions about the world around you. You try to answer your questions by doing investigations.

Some investigations are simple, such as watching animals play. Other investigations take planning. You need to gather and set up materials. Then you write down what happens.

You can think like a scientist on your own or in a group. Sharing what you learn is part of the fun. So get started!

Why does a compass point north?

What do stars look like through a telescope?

What Do You See?

So you want to think like a scientist? Let's get started. Try making some observations and inferences!

Active Reading As you read these two pages, find and underline the definition of *observe*.

Look at the pictures on this page. What do you see? When you use your senses to notice details, you **observe**.

Things you observe can start you thinking. Look at the picture of the small sailboat. You see that it has more than one sail. Now look more closely. The sails are different shapes and sizes.

You might infer that the shape or size of the sails affects how the boat moves. When you **infer**, you offer an explanation of what you observed. You might infer that each sail helps the boat move in a different way.

Make an observation about this boat.

_____

_____

_____

© Houghton Mifflin Harcourt Publishing Company (r) (l) iStock/Alamy (t) (l) Matthias Kulka/Corbis

Make an observation about this ship.

_____

_____

CONTAINER SHIP

Make an observation about this boat.

_____

_____

623 U.S. COAST GUARD

Write an inference based on this observation:
"I can see the wind blowing this sail."

_____

_____

Getting Answers!

People ask questions all day long. But not all questions are science questions. Science questions can be answered in many ways.

Active Reading As you read these two pages, circle a common, everyday word that has a different meaning in science.

Exploring

Some science questions can be answered by exploring. Say you see a leaf float by on the water. You wonder what else can float on water. You find an eraser in your pocket. You **predict**, or use what you know to tell if it will sink or float. When you know which items float and which don't, you can **classify**, or group, them.

Predict

Think about each item pictured. Then circle the ones you predict will float. Mark an *X* on those you predict will sink.

Investigating

You might think of an investigation as looking for clues. In science, an **investigation** is a planned way of finding answers to questions. When you do an investigation, you might ask a cause-and-effect question, "Does the amount of weight in a boat affect whether it floats or sinks?" Because you don't want to use a real boat, you can **make and use models.** A raft made of sticks is not exactly like a real boat, but it can be used to learn about them.

Investigating Answers

There are many steps a scientist may take during an investigation. Some do all five described here.

Active Reading As you read these two pages, number the sentences that describe Onisha's experiment to match the numbered steps in the circles.

1 Ask a Question

What causes things to change? This is the kind of question you can answer with an investigation.

2 Hypothesize

A **hypothesis** is a statement that could answer your question. You must be able to test a hypothesis.

3 Predict and Plan an Investigation

Predict what you will observe if your hypothesis is correct. **Identify the variable** to test, and keep other variables the same.

What Onisha Did …

Onisha thought about rafts floating down a river. She asked a question, "Does the size of a raft affect the amount of weight it can carry?"

Onisha **hypothesizes** that a bigger raft can carry more weight. Then she predicted, "I should be able to add more weight to a bigger raft than to a smaller raft." Onisha planned an investigation called an experiment. Outside of science, experimenting means trying something new, such as a new recipe. In science, an **experiment** is a test done to gather evidence. The evidence might support the hypothesis, or it might not. In her experiment, Onisha built three model rafts that differed only in their number of planks. She carefully put one penny at a time onto each raft until it sank. She recorded her results and drew a conclusion.

Variable

The factor that is changed in an experiment is called a **variable**. It's important to change only one variable at a time.

Draw Conclusions

Analyze your results, and **draw a conclusion.** Ask yourself, "Do the results support my hypothesis?" Share your conclusion with others.

4

Experiment

Now do the experiment to test your hypothesis.

5

▶ What was the variable in Onisha's experiment?

_____

_____

Sum It Up!

When you're done, use the answer key to check and revise your work.

Write words from the lesson that match the pictures.

2 _____

1 _____

The small plane will fly farther.

3 _____

4 _____

Use what you learned from the lesson to fill in the sequence below.

observe

5 _____

6 _____

7 _____

Answer Key: 1. use models 2. variable 3. investigate 4. predict 5. infer 6. hypothesize 7. experiment

Name _____

Word Play

1 Use the words in the box to complete the puzzle.

Across

1. You do this when you make a conclusion after observing.
5. the one factor you change in an experiment
6. to make a guess based on what you know or think
8. something that is like the real thing—but not exactly
9. a statement that will answer a question you want to investigate

Down

1. Scientists plan and carry one out to answer their questions.
2. Scientists ask these about the world around them.
3. You do this when you use your five senses.
4. an investigation in which you use variables
7. You draw this at the end of an investigation.

experiment*   infer*   **questions**   investigation*   variable*   hypothesis*

predict*   **model**   observe*   **conclusion**

* Key Lesson Vocabulary

Apply Concepts

2 This bridge is over the Mississippi River. List materials you could use to make a model of it.

_____

_____

3 Greyson wants to know what plants need in order to survive. He places one plant in a window. He places another plant in a dark closet. What is the variable he is testing?

_____

4 Jared looks carefully at a young turtle in his hand. Label each of his statements *observation* or *inference*.

Its front legs are longer than its back legs. _____

It has sharp toenails. _____

It uses its toenails to dig. _____

It can see me. _____

Its shell feels cool and dry against

my hand. _____

See *ScienceSaurus*® for more information about questions.

Inquiry Flipchart p. 3

Name _____

Essential Question

How Can You Use a Model?

Set a Purpose
What is the question you will try to answer with this investigation?

_____

_____

_____

State Your Hypothesis
Write your hypothesis, or idea you will test.

_____

_____

_____

Think About the Procedure
What is the variable you plan to test?

_____

_____

How will you know whether the variable you changed worked?

_____

_____

_____

Record Your Results
Fill in the chart to record how far the plane flew each time you changed its design.

Change Made to the Model	Distance It Flew

Draw Conclusions

1. Which changes to your model worked best?

_____

_____

_____

_____

2. Was your hypothesis supported by the results? How do you know?

_____

_____

Analyze and Extend

1. How is your model the same as a real airplane?

_____

_____

2. What did you learn about real airplanes from using a model?

_____

_____

_____

3. How is your model different from a real airplane?

_____

_____

_____

_____

4. What can't you learn about real airplanes by using a paper airplane?

_____

_____

_____

_____

5. Think of another question you would like to answer about airplane models.

_____

_____

_____

Essential Question

How Do Scientists Use Tools?

Engage Your Brain!

A hand lens can make a bug look bigger.

What other tools make objects look bigger?

_____

_____

_____

Active Reading

Lesson Vocabulary

List each term. As you learn about each one, make notes in the Interactive Glossary.

_____

_____

_____

Compare and Contrast

Ideas in parts of this lesson explain comparisons and contrasts—they tell how things are alike and different. Active readers focus on comparisons and contrasts when they ask questions such as, How are measuring tools alike and different?

Make It Clear!

Scientists use tools to give them super-vision!
Some tools that do this include hand lenses
and microscopes.

Active Reading As you read these two pages, circle words or phrases that signal when things are alike and different.

Light microscopes let you see
tiny objects by using a light
source and lenses or mirrors
inside the microscope.

A magnifying box
has a lens in its lid.

A hand lens has one
lens with a handle.

Use forceps to pick up tiny objects
to view with magnifiers.

Use a dropper to move small
amounts of liquids for viewing.

Close, Closer, Closest!

Magnifying tools make objects look larger. Hold a hand lens close to one eye. Then move the hand lens closer to the object until it looks large and sharp. A magnifying box is like a hand lens in that it also has one lens. You can put things that are hard to hold, such as a bug, in it.

A **microscope** magnifies objects that are too tiny to be seen with the eye alone. Its power is much greater than that of a hand lens or magnifying box. Most microscopes have two or more lenses that work together.

▶ Draw a picture of how something you see might look if it was magnified.

Pond water as seen with just your eyes.

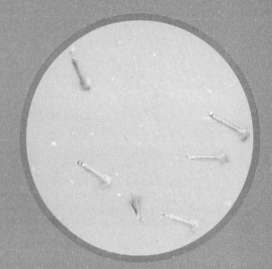

Pond water as seen through a hand lens.

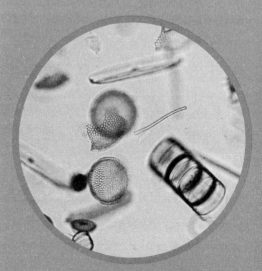

Pond water as seen through a microscope.

19

Measure It!

Measuring uses numbers to describe the world around you. There are several ways to measure and more than one tool or unit for each way.

Active Reading As you read the next page, circle the main idea.

A balance has a pan on either side. Put the object you want to measure on one pan and add masses to the other pan until they are balanced. The basic unit of mass is the gram.

The units on measuring tapes can be centimeters and meters or inches and feet.

ruler

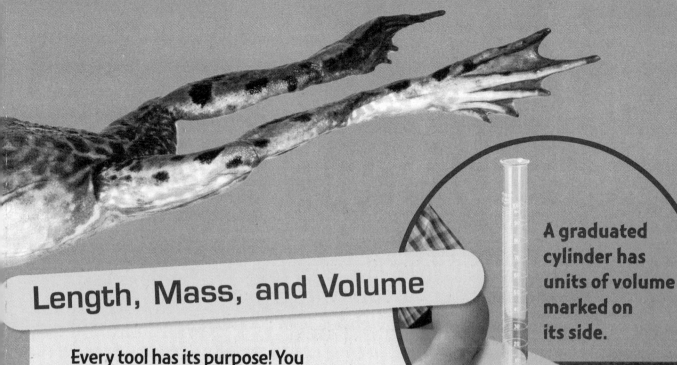

A graduated cylinder has units of volume marked on its side.

Length, Mass, and Volume

Every tool has its purpose! You can **measure** length with rulers and tape measures. Mass is the amount of matter in an object. It is measured with a pan balance. Volume is the amount of space a solid, liquid, or gas takes up.

The volume of a liquid can be measured with a **graduated cylinder** or a measuring cup or spoon. You can also use these tools to find the volume of solids that can be poured, such as sugar or salt. You **use numbers** to report measurements and **compare** objects. You can also **order** things using measurements. You can put pencils in order from shortest to longest.

Measuring cups and spoons are used because the amount of each ingredient is very important.

Do the Math!
Subtract Units

Use a metric ruler to measure the parts of the frog.

1. How many centimeters is the frog's longest front leg?

   _____

2. How many centimeters is the frog's longest back leg?

   _____

3. Now find the difference.

   _____

4. Compare your measurements to those of other students.

   _____

   _____

Time and Temperature

How long did that earthquake shake? Which freezes faster, hot water or cold water? Scientists need tools to answer these questions!

Time

When you count the steady drip of a leaky faucet, you are thinking about time. You can **use time and space relationships.** Clocks and stopwatches are tools that measure time. The base unit of time is the second. One minute is equal to 60 seconds. One hour is equal to 60 minutes.

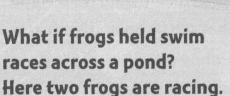

What if frogs held swim races across a pond? Here two frogs are racing.

START!

Temperature

When you say that ovens are hot or freezers are cold, you are thinking about **temperature**. A thermometer is the tool used to measure temperature. The base units of temperature are called degrees, but all degrees are not the same.

Scientists usually measure temperature in degrees Celsius. Most people around the world use Celsius, too. In the United States, however, degrees Fahrenheit are used to report the weather, body temperature, and in cooking.

▶ The first frog finished the race in 19 seconds. The second frog finished the race in 47 seconds. How much more quickly did the winning frog finish the race?

_____

_____

_____

How Do You Care for Tropical Fish?

To care for tropical fish, you have to think like a scientist and use science tools.

Close Encounters

A public aquarium [uh•KWAIR•ee•uhm] is the place to see sharks and tropical fish. That's where many people get excited about keeping tropical fish at home. The word *aquarium* is used for both the big place you visit and the small tank in your home. Caring for both takes similar skills: observing, inferring, measuring, and recording data.

Does moving your aquarium in front of the window change the water's temperature?

What is the volume of water in your aquarium?

Keep Good Records

Keeping good records is important, whether you're recording data in your Science Notebook or making entries in your aquarium log. In your log, record the temperature every time you check it. Write the time you feed the fish and the volume of food you give them. Making correct measurements is part of being a good scientist.

Water test kits identify materials in the water.

Taking care of fish means checking the temperature.

Cause and Effect

Every change in an aquarium has a cause. Sometimes fish in an aquarium might become sick. Think of two things that might cause the fish to get sick.

_____

_____

_____

Sum It Up!

When you're done, use the answer key to check and revise your work.

The idea web below summarizes this lesson. Complete the web.

How Scientists Use Tools

1 They use hand lenses and microscopes to make things look

_____.

They use tools to measure.

2 Length is measured with

_____

_____.

3 A graduated cylinder measures

_____.

4 Pan balances measure

_____.

5 They measure time with clocks and

_____.

Brain Check

Name _____

Word Play

1 Write each term after its definition. Then find each term in the word search puzzle.

A. A tool used to measure mass _____

B. A temperature scale used by scientists _____

C. A tool used to pick up tiny objects _____

D. A tool used to measure volume _____

E. A tool you hold against your eye to make objects look bigger

_____

F. How hot or cold something is _____

G. A tool that measures temperature _____

H. Something you measure with a stopwatch _____

I. How much space something takes up _____

```
L  T  E  M  P  E  R  A  T  U  R  E  R  M  Y  O  L
U  H  R  P  A  M  I  L  C  E  L  S  I  U  S  V  W
K  E  E  A  V  S  U  N  B  O  W  L  M  A  X  Y  M
N  R  V  N  U  O  M  Z  O  O  L  I  S  S  T  F  O
G  M  C  B  E  U  L  I  H  T  M  A  Y  T  L  O  K
Y  O  Y  A  B  L  U  U  M  I  M  M  Y  O  R  R  J
F  M  S  L  K  K  Z  W  M  M  X  Q  I  P  Z  C  D
K  E  H  A  R  O  O  R  L  E  A  F  S  I  M  E  E
E  T  N  N  R  U  C  L  M  K  P  I  U  T  X  P  H
S  E  N  C  F  I  L  L  H  A  N  D  L  E  N  S  S
J  R  U  E  M  M  U  V  L  V  I  G  T  H  M  I  T
G  R  A  D  U  A  T  E  D  C  Y  L  I  N  D  E  R
```

Apply Concepts

In 2–5, tell which tool(s) you would use and how you would use them.

 thermometer

 measuring spoons

 measuring tape   ruler

 magnifying box

2 Find out how long your dog is from nose to tail.

_____

_____

_____

3 Decide if you need to wear a sweatshirt outdoors.

_____

_____

_____

4 Make a bubble bath that has just the right amount of bubbles and is not too hot or too cold.

_____

_____

_____

_____

5 Examine a ladybug and count its legs without hurting it.

_____

_____

_____

_____

 **Take It Home!**

Share what you have learned about measuring with your family. With a family member, identify examples of objects you could measure in or near your home.

Name _____

Essential Question

How Can You Measure Length?

Set a Purpose
What will you be able to do at the end of this investigation?

_____

_____

_____

_____

Think About the Procedure
What will you think about when choosing the measurement tool for each item?

_____

_____

_____

How will you choose the units that are best for each item?

_____

_____

_____

Record Your Results
In the space below, make a table in which you record your measurements.

29

Draw Conclusions

1. How does choosing the best tool make measuring length easier?

_____

_____

_____

_____

_____

2. How do units affect the quality of a measurement?

_____

_____

_____

_____

Analyze and Extend

1. Did groups who used the same tools as your group get the same results as you? Explain why or why not.

_____

_____

_____

2. Why was it important to communicate your results with other groups? Explain.

_____

_____

_____

3. When would someone want to use millimeters to find out who throws a ball the farthest? When would using millimeters not be a good choice? (1,000 mm = 1 m)

_____

_____

_____

4. Think of another question you would like to ask about measuring.

_____

_____

_____

Materials
Which tools should you use?

Garter snake

Hemlock tree cone

Ladybug beetle

Bird's feather

31

Essential Question

How Do Scientists Use Data?

Engage Your Brain!

People sometimes make statues out of blocks. If you could count how many blocks of each color there are, how would you record this information?

_____

_____

_____

_____

Active Reading

Lesson Vocabulary

List each term. As you learn about each one, make notes in the Interactive Glossary.

_____   _____

_____   _____

_____   _____

_____

Main Ideas

The main idea of a section is the most important idea. The main idea may be stated in the first sentence, or it may be stated elsewhere. Active readers look for main ideas by asking themselves, What is this section mostly about?

Show Me the Evidence

Scientists use observations to answer their questions. You can do this, too!

Active Reading As you read these two pages, find and underline the definitions of *data* and *evidence*.

My data are my *evidence*. The data show that a raft with six planks floats twice as much weight as a raft with three planks.

Onisha, how do you know that a bigger raft can float more weight than a smaller one?

- I put the pennies on the raft with three planks. It held fewer pennies than the other raft.

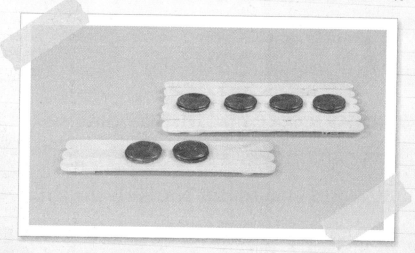

Each science observation is a piece of **data.** For example, the number of pennies on a raft is data.

Onisha finished her investigation and thought about what it meant. She studied her data. Scientists use data as **evidence** to decide whether a hypothesis is or is not supported. Either way, scientists learn valuable things.

Scientists ask other scientists a lot of questions. They compare data. They repeat the investigation to see if they get the same results. Scientists review and talk about the evidence. They agree and disagree while respecting each other's ideas.

▶ Scientists might live too far away to meet face to face. What are three other ways they can share data and discuss evidence?

_____

_____

_____

_____

_____

_____

_____

_____

Communicating Data

Scientists record and display data so others can understand it. There are many ways and many tools to do this.

How can I communicate my results?

Models can help us understand things that are too big, small, or dangerous to do or observe.

▶ You want to find how high different kinds of balls bounce. You test each ball 20 times. How will you record and display your measurements?

_____

_____

After you **gather data**, you can share, or **communicate**, it with others in different ways. How can you **record data**? To show how birds get seeds from a feeder, you can use a camera. If you observe how a dog cares for her puppies, write in a journal.

Sometimes scientists use charts and graphs to help **interpret** and **display data**. A **chart** is a display that organizes data into rows and columns. A **data table** is a kind of chart for recording numbers. A **bar graph** is used to compare data about different events or groups. Bar graphs make it easier to see patterns or relationships in data.

These students made a bar graph and a data table to compare results.

Maps, like this world map, help to show the relationships between different objects or ideas.

▶ You want to show kinds of weather in different places. How could you display this information?

_____

_____

▶ You want to show the different layers that make up Earth's crust. What could you use?

_____

_____

How To Do It!

What are some ways to display data? You can use data tables, bar graphs, and line graphs. How can students use displays to show what they observed in the butterfly garden?

DATA TABLE

Month	Number of Butterflies
March	5
April	5
May	9
June	14

BAR GRAPH

Butterfly Garden

How do you create a graph? First, look at the data table. Each column has a heading telling what information is in that column. Now, look at the graphs. Did you notice that the same headings are used to name the parts of the graphs?

On the graphs, look at the line next to the heading "Number of Butterflies." It looks like a number line, starting at zero and getting larger. It shows the number of butterflies.

To complete the bar graph, find the name of a month along the bottom. Then, move your finger up until you reach the number of butterflies for that month. Draw a bar to that point. To complete the line graph, draw points to show the number of butterflies for each month. Then, connect the points.

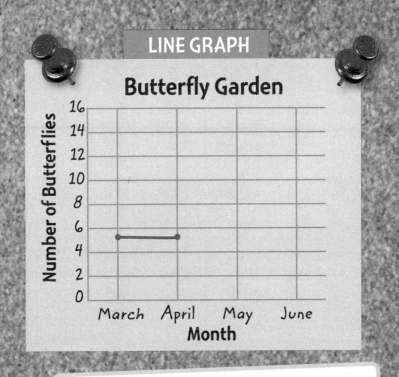

LINE GRAPH

Butterfly Garden

▶ Now it's your turn. Use the data table to help you complete the graphs for the months of May and June.

Why Graphs?

Sharing information with others is important to scientists. How do graphs help us share?

I can share these results with other scientists. They can repeat the experiment to see if they get different results.

Why did you use a graph instead of a data table?

A graph helps you see information quickly and recognize patterns.

DATA TABLE

Class	Number of Cans
Room 5	40
Room 8	55
Room 11	20
Room 12	35
Room 15	45

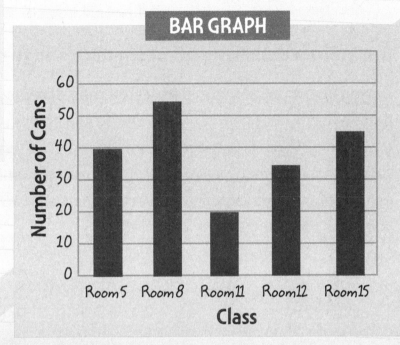

BAR GRAPH

Do the Math!
Interpret a Graph

Students collected evidence about a canned food drive in a data table. They organized the data in a graph.

1. Use the data table to find which class brought the least number of cans.

_____

2. Use the graph to find which class brought the greatest number of cans.

_____

3. Which was easier to use, the data table or the graph? Why?

_____

_____

_____

_____

_____

_____

_____

Sum It Up!

When you're done, use the answer key to check
and revise your work.

Use information in the summary to complete the graphic organizer.

During investigations scientists record their observations, or
data. When other scientists ask, "How do you know?", they
explain how their data supports their answers. Observations
can be shared in many ways. Data in the form of numbers
can be shown in data tables and bar graphs. Data can also be
shared as models, maps, or in writing.

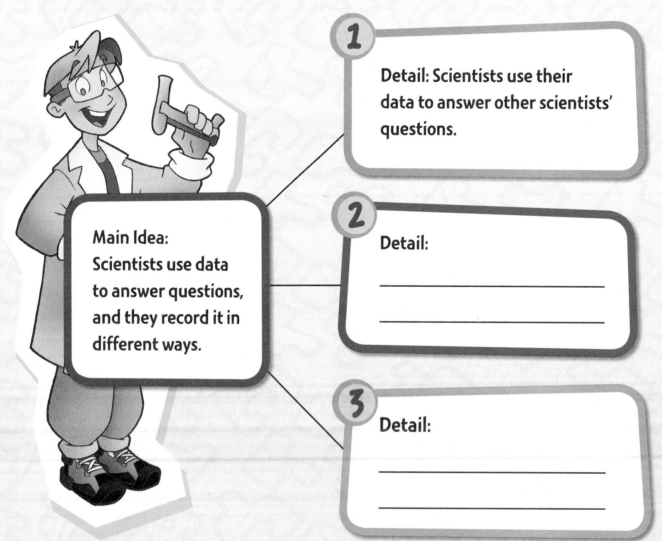

Main Idea:
Scientists use data
to answer questions,
and they record it in
different ways.

1 Detail: Scientists use their
data to answer other scientists'
questions.

2 Detail:
_____
_____

3 Detail:
_____
_____

Answer Key: 2. Data can be shown in data tables and bar graphs, 3. Data can also be
shared as models, maps, or in writing.

Name _____

Word Play

Find the correct meaning and underline it.

1 Data
- tools used to measure
- steps in an investigation
- pieces of scientific information

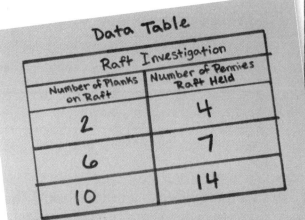

2 Evidence
- a kind of graph
- how much space something takes up
- the facts that show if a hypothesis is correct

3 Data table
- a chart for recording numbers
- the number of planks on a raft
- a piece of furniture used by scientists

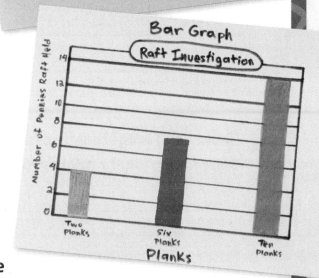

4 Bar graph
- a chart for recording numbers
- a graph in the shape of a circle
- a graph that shows how things compare

5 Communicate
- take a photograph
- share data with others
- collect and record data

Apply Concepts

Read the paragraph and answer questions 6–7.

One morning, your dad walks you and your sister to the school bus stop. When you get there, you wonder, "Has the bus come yet?"

6 What evidence would support the idea that the bus has not arrived yet?

_____

_____

7 What evidence would support the idea that the bus had already come?

_____

_____

_____

8 Your friend brags that he can throw a baseball 100 meters. What evidence would prove this?

_____

_____

_____

Take It Home!

Share with your family what you have learned about recording evidence. With a family member, identify something you want to observe. Then decide how to record your data.

© Houghton Mifflin Harcourt Publishing Company   (tr) ©Pauline St. Denis/Corbis; (br) ©Purestock/Alamy

Inquiry Flipchart p. 7

Name _____

Essential Question

How Do Your Results Compare?

Set a Purpose
What will you learn from this investigation?

_____

_____

State Your Hypothesis
Tell how you think the height of bubbles in water relates to the amount of dishwashing liquid used.

_____

_____

_____

Think About the Procedure
List the things you did that were the same each time.

_____

_____

_____

Describe the variable, the one thing you changed each time.

_____

_____

_____

Record Data
In the space below, make a table to record your measurements.

Draw Conclusions

Look back at your hypothesis. Did your results support it? Explain your answer.

_____

_____

_____

_____

Analyze and Extend

1. Why is it helpful to compare results with others?

_____

_____

_____

_____

2. What would you do if you found out that your results were very different from those of others?

_____

_____

_____

3. The bar graph below shows the height of the column of bubbles produced by equal amounts of three brands of dishwashing liquid. What does this data show?

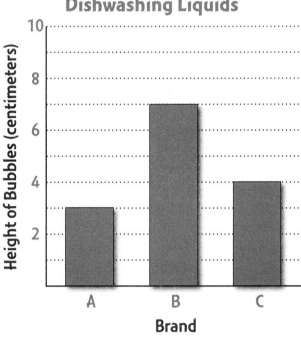

Bubbles Made by Dishwashing Liquids

_____

_____

_____

_____

_____

4. Think of other questions you would like to ask about bubbles.

_____

_____

_____

_____

1 A meteorologist is a person who studies weather.

2 Meteorologists use tools to measure temperature, wind speed, and air pressure.

6 THINGS

You Should Know About

Meteorologists

3 Meteorologists use data they collect to forecast the weather.

4 Computers help meteorologists share weather data from around the world.

5 Keeping good records helps meteorologists see weather patterns.

6 Meteorologists' forecasts help people stay safe during bad weather.

Careers in Science continued

Be a Meteorologist

Answer the questions below using the Weather Forecast bar graph.

1 What was the temperature on Thursday? _____

2 Which day was cloudy and rainy? _____

3 How much cooler was it on Tuesday than Thursday? _____

4 Which day was partly cloudy? _____

5 Compare the temperatures on Tuesday and Friday. Which day had the higher temperature? _____

6 In the forecast below, which day has the highest temperature? _____ The lowest? _____

WEATHER FORECAST

Temperature °F — Monday, Tuesday, Wednesday, Thursday, Friday

Day of week

48

Unit 1 Review

Vocabulary Review

Use the terms in the box to complete the sentences.

> bar graph
> evidence
> experiment
> hypothesis
> variable

1. You can share the results of an investigation with others by using a(n) _____.

2. An observation often leads to a testable question known as a(n) _____.

3. A test done to gather evidence is called a(n) _____.

4. It is very important to test only one _____, or thing that changes, at a time.

5. A hypothesis should be supported by the _____.

Science Concepts

Fill in the letter of the choice that best answers the question.

6. Alix wants to conduct an experiment to find out how fertilizer affects bean plants. Which of the following is a hypothesis that she could test?

   (A) Alix will need bean seeds, soil, fertilizer, and water.

   (B) All the plants must get the same amount of sunlight.

   (C) Fertilizer can be organic or chemical.

   (D) Fertilizer causes bean plants to grow larger and faster.

7. Samuel noticed that small dogs often have a high-pitched bark, while big dogs often have a low-pitched bark. Would a scientist consider this an experiment?

   (A) Yes, because you could study many different sizes and types of dogs to find out if it is true.

   (B) Yes, because there may be a scientific reason for the difference in dog barks.

   (C) No, because this is an observation, not an experiment.

   (D) No, because it is illegal to use experiments to learn about animals.

Science Concepts

Fill in the letter of the choice that best answers the question.

8. Zelia performed an experiment to see if a toy car would travel down a ramp faster on wax paper or sandpaper. For each type of surface, she timed how long it took for the same toy car to reach the bottom of the ramp. Her results are shown in the table.

	Wax paper	Sandpaper
Trial 1	8 seconds	12 seconds
Trial 2	7 seconds	11 seconds
Trial 3	8 seconds	23 seconds
Trial 4	9 seconds	13 seconds

Which trial has most likely been recorded incorrectly?

- (A) Trial 1
- (B) Trial 2
- (C) Trial 3
- (D) Trial 4

9. A tool often used in science is shown below.

For which task would this tool most likely be used?

- (A) observing bread mold closely
- (B) observing the color of a leaf
- (C) observing planets in the solar system
- (D) observing the texture of a rock

10. Gabe is interested in animals that live in the desert. He wants to learn more about what desert animals eat. Which of these should Gabe use in his investigation?

- (A) a model of a desert animal
- (B) a chart showing monthly rainfall in the desert
- (C) a data table showing food for desert animals
- (D) a graph of average temperatures in the desert

11. The picture below shows a tool used for measuring liquids.

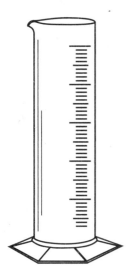

Which could this tool measure?

(A) mass

(B) length

(C) temperature

(D) volume

12. Ranjit wants to build shelves in a closet. The closet is 2 meters wide. The wooden boards he wants to use are more than 2 meters long. He will need to measure the boards, then use a saw to cut the correct length. What tool should Ranjit use to measure the correct length of the boards?

(A) a balance

(B) a pedometer

(C) a tape measure

(D) a graduated cylinder

13. Martina is investigating how different types of soil affect radish seed germination. She plans to plant the same number of radish seeds in three different types of soil. Each day for a week, she will count the number of radish seeds that emerge from the soil. What should Martina use to collect and organize her information?

(A) a model

(B) a data table

(C) a stopwatch

(D) a thermometer

14. Zane is doing an experiment in which he measures the temperature of the water in three different tanks. Which of the following tools would he use?

(A) a thermometer

(B) a pan balance

(C) a microscope

(D) a stopwatch

Apply Inquiry and Review the Big Idea

Write the answers to these questions.

15. This picture shows a model of the sun, Earth, and Earth's moon.

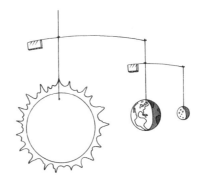

What is the advantage of using a model like the one shown?

_____

_____

16. Luisa was studying whether certain tropical flowers would bloom even when temperatures dropped below 15 degrees Celsius. She placed the blooming plants outside. She measured the temperature outside each day for seven days. She observed that the plants bloomed each day of the week. The graph shows the data she collected.

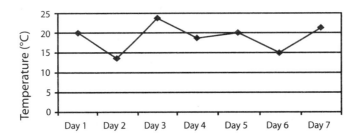

What is one conclusion Luisa could draw based on the data in her graph?

_____

_____

17. Two teams measured the mass and the volume of the same rubber duck. One team found the mass to be 65 g and the volume to be 150 mL. The other team found that the mass was 63 g and the volume was 149 mL. What could explain these differences?

_____

_____

UNIT 2
The Engineering Process

Union Station in
Indianapolis, Indiana

Big Idea

Technology is all around us. The design process is used to develop new types of technology to meet people's needs.

I Wonder Why

This building was built in 1853. How has the building process changed since then? Stayed the same? *Turn the page to find out.*

Here's Why In 1853, tools were less complex than they are today, and they were not electric. But today's builders still have to draw plans, choose materials, and make sure the building is safe to use.

In this unit, you will explore the Big Idea, the Essential Questions, and the Investigations on the Inquiry Flipchart.

Levels of Inquiry Key ■ DIRECTED ■ GUIDED ■ INDEPENDENT

Big Idea Technology is all around us. The design process is used to develop new types of technology to meet people's needs.

Essential Questions

Now I Get the Big Idea!

Science Notebook

Before you begin each lesson, be sure to write your thoughts about the Essential Question.

Essential Question

How Do Engineers Use the Design Process?

Engage Your Brain!

Designs solve problems. What problem does the bridge solve?

_____

_____

Active Reading

Lesson Vocabulary

List the term. As you learn about it, make notes in the Interactive Glossary.

_____

Problem-Solution

Ideas in this lesson may be connected by a problem-solution relationship. Active readers mark a problem with a *P* to help them stay focused on the way information is organized. When solutions are described, active readers mark each solution with an *S*.

The Design Process

To get to school, you may have ridden your bike or taken the bus. These are two different ways of getting to school, but they have something in common.

Active Reading As you read this page, circle the five steps of the design process and number each step.

Both of the methods of transportation above were developed by someone who used the design process. The **design process** is the process engineers follow to solve problems. It is a multistep process that includes finding a problem, planning and building, testing and improving, redesigning, and communicating results.

The William H. Natcher Bridge makes crossing the Ohio River easy and fast!

An engineer used the design process to design the supports for this bridge.

The design process can help people solve problems or design creative solutions. Look at the picture of the Ohio River between Rockport, Indiana, and Owensboro, Kentucky. In the past, only one bridge connected these cities. Over time, the bridge got very crowded. In this lesson, you'll see how the design process was used to design a solution to this problem.

How Do Inventions Help You?

Think of an invention that has made your life easier. What problem did it solve? How do you think the inventor used the design process to find the solution?

_____

_____

_____

_____

_____

Finding
a Problem

The design process starts with finding a problem. An engineer can't design a solution without first knowing what the problem is!

Active Reading As you read these two pages, put brackets [ ] around sentences that describe the problem, and write *P* in front of the brackets. Put brackets around sentences that describe the steps toward a solution, and write *S* in front of the brackets.

A team of scientists and engineers worked together. They saw there was a lot of traffic on the old bridge. People of both cities needed another way to cross the Ohio River. The team studied the best way to get the most people and cars across the river.

© Houghton Mifflin Harcourt Publishing Company (bkgd) © Credit: SonjaBK/iStock/Getty Images

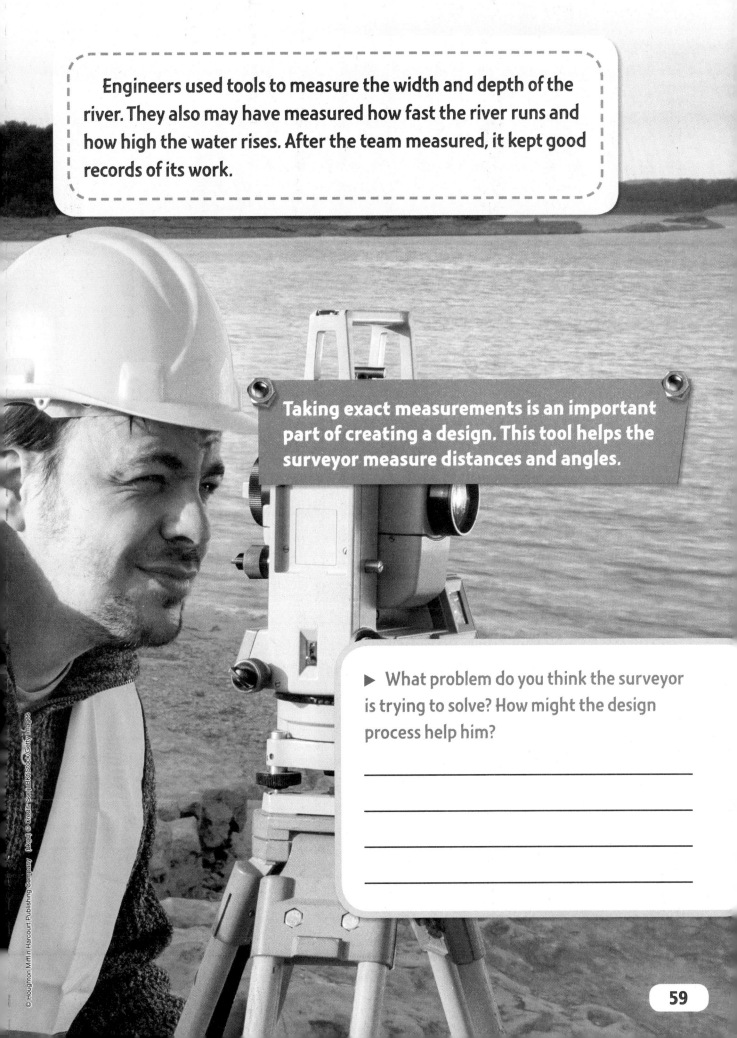

Engineers used tools to measure the width and depth of the river. They also may have measured how fast the river runs and how high the water rises. After the team measured, it kept good records of its work.

Taking exact measurements is an important part of creating a design. This tool helps the surveyor measure distances and angles.

▶ What problem do you think the surveyor is trying to solve? How might the design process help him?

_____

_____

_____

_____

Planning and Building

The team decided the best solution would be to build another bridge across the Ohio River.

Active Reading As you read these two pages, underline the sentences that describe steps in the design process.

The next step in the design process is to test and improve the prototype. The engineers gather data about important features of the bridge design, such as how stable it is and how much weight it can support. The team may modify minor aspects of the design based on this data.

If the data show that the prototype has significant flaws, the team must start over again. They redesign the bridge by making major changes to their initial plan.

Engineers carefully evaluated and tested the safety of the William H. Natcher Bridge. They made sure that builders followed the plans and used the correct materials.

The last step in the design process is to communicate the solution. Bridge inspectors used their findings, or evidence, to write reports. They used mathematical representations, such as graphs, tables, and drawings, to explain that the bridge was safe to open. Engineers could now use this information to make improvements and build bridges in other places!

The prototype helped builders know how wide, tall, and long to make the bridge.

Communication Is Key!

List three other ways you might communicate the results of a project to others.

_____

_____

How Do Designs Get Better Over Time?

An engineer's work is never done! Every invention can be improved. For example, instead of building a fire in a wood stove or turning on a gas or electric oven, you can use a microwave to cook your food.

Just as with stoves, engineers have come up with newer and better designs for cell phones. Forty years ago, cell phones were bulky and heavy. Today, the smallest cell phone is not much bigger than a watch!

Martin Cooper invented the first cell phone in 1973. It was 13 inches long, weighed about 2 pounds, and allowed only 30 minutes of talk time.

► What might happen if cell phones get too small?

_____

_____

_____

Cell phones today do much more than just make phone calls. They let you take pictures, look up directions, listen to music, watch TV, or search the Internet.

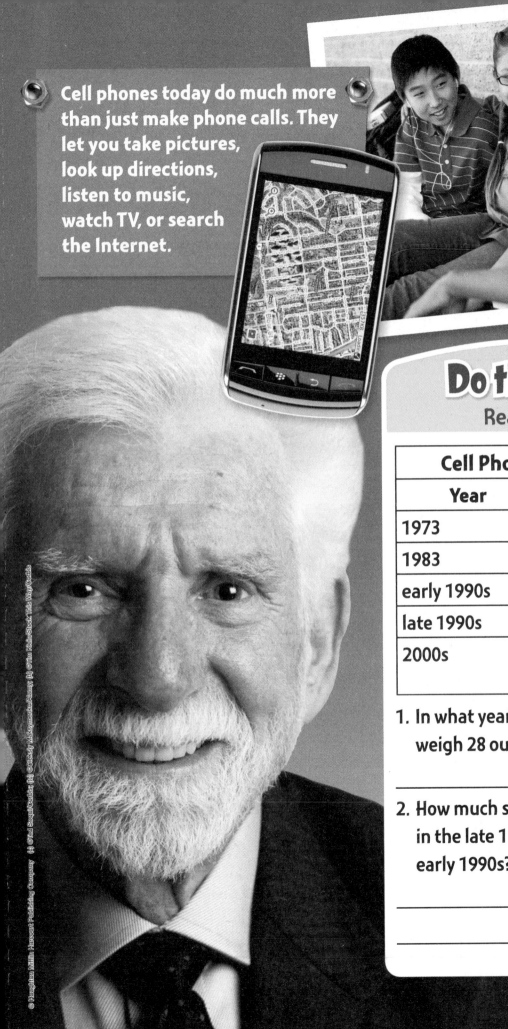

Do the Math!
Read a Table

Cell Phones Over Time	
Year	**Weight**
1973	about 2 pounds
1983	28 ounces
early 1990s	about 8 ounces
late 1990s	about 4 ounces
2000s	less than 2 ounces

1. In what year did cell phones weigh 28 ounces?

_____

2. How much smaller were phones in the late 1990s than in the early 1990s?

_____

_____

Sum It Up!

When you're done, use the answer key to check and revise your work.

Complete the step of the design process in each sentence.

1

1. First, find a _____ .

2. Second, _____ and _____ a prototype.

3. Third, _____ and _____ the prototype.

4. Fourth, _____ the prototype as necessary.

5. Fifth, _____ the solution, test data, and your improvements.

Answer Key: 1. problem 2. plan, build 3. test, improve 4. redesign 5. communicate

Brain Check

Name _____

Word Play

1 Use these words to complete the puzzle.

Across

2. A plan for a solution that may use many drawings
6. A way of letting people know about a design

Down

1. Something that needs a solution
3. The steps engineers follow to solve problems
4. To judge how well a design works
5. The outcome of the design process

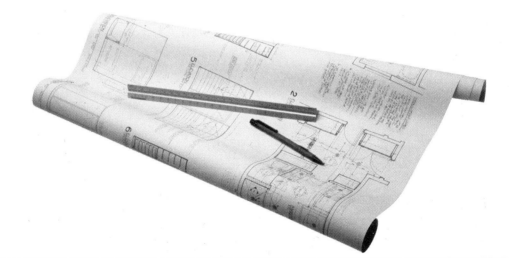

problem   process   solution   design   evaluate   communicate

Apply Concepts

2 Kyle's guinea pig is curious! It always finds a way out of its cage. Use the design process to help Kyle solve this problem.

_____

_____

_____

_____

_____

3 Label each of the following as a problem or a solution.

_____ _____ _____ _____

See *ScienceSaurus*® for more information about engineers.

Take It Home!

Name _____

Essential Question

How Can You Design a Tree House?

Set a Purpose
What will you do in this activity?

_____

_____

_____

_____

State Your Hypothesis
What parts of the design process will you use in this activity?

_____

_____

_____

_____

Think About the Procedure
Why is it important to have a plan before you start building the tree house?

_____

_____

_____

_____

_____

_____

What problems do you identify? How might you solve these problems?

_____

_____

_____

_____

_____

_____

_____

Record Your Data

In the space below, draw a prototype for your plan.

[blank box for drawing]

Draw Conclusions

Why do you think it is important to build a prototype for your plan before you start building the actual tree house?

_____

_____

_____

_____

Analyze and Extend

1. Suppose you were going to use the design process to build the tree house you've designed. What more would you need to do before you began building?

_____

_____

_____

2. As you look at your prototype and think about it, is there any part you would want to redesign? Why?

_____

_____

_____

_____

_____

_____

_____

_____

3. What other things would you like to know about how the design process is used to plan projects like your tree house?

_____

_____

_____

_____

_____

_____

_____

Essential Question

How Are Technology and Society Related?

Engage Your Brain!

Find the answer to the following question in this lesson and record it here.

Where is the technology in this picture?

_____

_____

_____

_____

_____

Active Reading

Lesson Vocabulary

Write the term. As you learn about it, make notes in the Interactive Glossary.

_____

Signal Words: Details

Signal words show connections between ideas. *For example* signals examples of an idea. *Also* signals added facts. Active readers remember what they read because they are alert to signal words that identify examples and facts about a topic.

Technology

What is technology? Look at this train station. Nearly everything you see is an example of technology.

Active Reading As you read these two pages, circle two clue words or phrases that signal a detail such as an example or an added fact.

Technology is anything that people make or do that changes the natural world. Technology meets people's wants or needs. Technology is not just computers and cell phones. Think about the things in a train station. They all have a purpose. The technology in a train station helps people travel easily. Can you imagine how different the world would be without technology?

Suitcase

A suitcase contains a traveler's needs. For example, it can carry clothing, shoes, pajamas, a hairbrush, a toothbrush, and toothpaste. All of these items are examples of technology.

Train Schedule Board

A schedule board tells when trains depart. It also names the track each train leaves on. This technology allows train schedules to be updated quickly as needed.

Clock

Clocks are also technology. They tell travelers what time it is. Travelers can tell how long it will be before their train arrives. They can also find out if they are late for their train.

INFORMATION

ATTENTION CUSTOMERS:
NEVER LEAVE PACKAGES UNATTENDED
UNATTENDED ITEMS MAY BE REMOVED
BY THE NTA POLICE DEPARTMENT.
THANK YOU FOR YOUR COOPERATION!

HARLEM LINE DEPA

TIME	TRK	DESTINATION	REMARKS
4:25	108	NO. WH PLAINS	FORDHAM -
4:48	17	SOUTHEAST	WHITE PLAIN
5:22	32	WASSAIC	WHITE PLAIN
5:25	105	NO. WH PLAINS	MELROSE -
5:40	17	SOUTHEAST	WHITE PLAIN

What Do Technologies Do?

List two technologies that you see in the photo. Tell what each does.

_____

_____

_____

Technology Through Time

A train today is different from a train from 100 years ago or even 50 years ago!

Steam locomotives were developed in the early 1800s. They were powered by burning wood or coal that heated water to make steam.

Active Reading As you read these two pages, draw two lines under the main idea.

Technology is always changing. The earliest trains were dragged along grooves in the ground. Today, superfast trains can travel hundreds of miles an hour. Train tracks have changed over time, too. New technology made tracks of iron. These could carry heavier loads. Trains could be larger and also travel faster. These improvements made trains more useful to people. Improvements in technology make trains work better, faster, and more easily.

Modern switches operate electronically. Computers send a signal that changes the tracks that the train will follow.

The earliest track switches were moved by hand.

Diesel engine 1900s

By the mid-1900s, the diesel engine had replaced the steam locomotive. Diesel is a type of fuel.

Maglev train 2000s

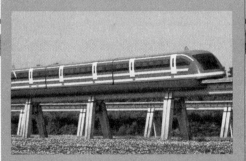

The fastest trains don't run on tracks anymore. Maglev trains ride on powerful magnets.

Do the Math!
Interpret a Table

Look at the table. How much faster is the Maglev train than the steam locomotive at maximum speed?

Train Speeds	
Train	Maximum speed (mph)
Steam locomotive	126
Diesel engine	100
Bullet Train	275
Maglev	361

_____

_____

_____

Technology and Society

Technology and society are connected. Technology affects how people live and what they do. People also affect technology by inventing new things.

Active Reading As you read these two pages, put brackets [ ] around the sentence that describes a problem and write *P* next to it. Underline the sentence that describes the solution and write *S* next to it.

Trains are an example of technology's connection to society. Trains carry people and cargo long distances. Resources, such as coal, can be carried long distances in a few days. Before trains, people in California may not have been able to get coal easily. People affect new train technology by finding ways for trains to cross high bridges or to tunnel through mountains. New technology helps trains meet people's needs and wants.

Some cities are far away from where coal is found and steel is produced. Train technology helps resources reach people in faraway cities.

Although trains through the Swiss Alps are safer than trucks on a road, only small trains can pass. The cars, roads, trains, and tracks are all transportation technologies that help people and goods move around the globe.

This new tunnel is beneath the Swiss Alps. The machine behind the workers is a technology that was used to help drill the tunnel. Large trains will be able to use the tunnel. Now people will be able to save more time traveling between cities.

Trains of the Future?

How would you change trains in the future? How would your changes affect society?

_____

_____

_____

_____

_____

Freight trains have refrigerator cars for keeping food fresh. This technology means that food can then be carried safely over long distances.

How Does Technology Affect You?

Technologies are always changing. Cars replaced horse-drawn carriages, and maybe someday flying cars will replace the cars we drive today!

Active Reading As you read this page, draw boxes around the names of the things that are being compared.

Think about the technology you use at school and at home. Have you noticed how they have changed? New televisions look different from older ones. Newer computers look much different, too. These newer technologies also do more than their older versions. Technology keeps improving with the goal of making life better.

Cell phone

Do you think when your grandparents were children they had the technology this boy has today?

Technology Changes

This camera uses film, which can store only about 20 images on a roll.

Digital cameras store hundreds of images. Images can be deleted for more space.

Cars in the 1960s used a lot of oil and gas and caused air pollution.

Hybrid cars use both electricity and gas to operate. They cause less air pollution.

Then and Now

Look at the technology below. What can you do with this technology today that people couldn't do 50 years ago?

Earlier telephones had rotary dials and were connected to the wall.

_____

_____

You could not easily edit your work on this typewriter.

_____

_____

Sum It Up!

When you're done, use the answer key to check and revise your work.

Complete the summary. Use the information to complete the graphic organizer.

Summarize

Technology is all around you. It can be very simple, like (1) _____.
At a train station, you may see a (2) _____ or a (3) _____.
If you live in a city you may see (4) _____ and (5) _____.
Even in your classroom at school you have a (6) _____, and you may even have a (7) _____.

Main Idea: Technology can be as simple as a fence or as complex as a space station.		
(8) Detail: Technology can be complex _____ _____ _____ _____	**(9) Detail:** Technology can be simple _____ _____ _____ _____	**Detail:** Technology can be simple, like a fence. 

78

Name _____

Word Play

1 Write four words from the box that are examples of technology.

fence	giraffe	cell phone	rock
horse	car	leaf	stove

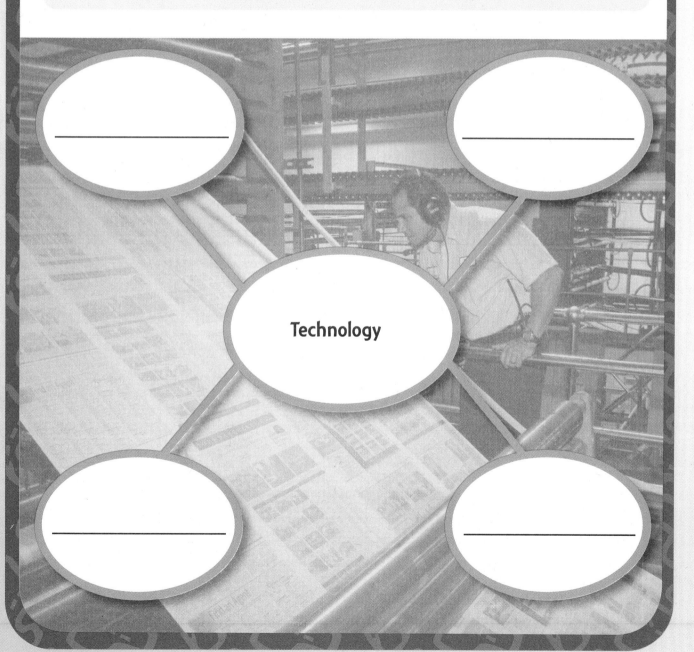

_____

_____

Technology

_____

_____

Apply Concepts

In 2–5, tell which technology you would use and how you would use it.

cell phone

magnifying glass

train

ruler

garden shovel

2 Get the lunch you left at home

_____

_____

_____

3 Visit a friend in another state

_____

_____

_____

4 Plant vegetables in your garden

_____

_____

_____

5 Find out what the fine print on a coupon says

_____

_____

_____

Take It Home!

Share what you have learned about technology with your family. With a family member, make a list of the technology in the kitchen of your home.

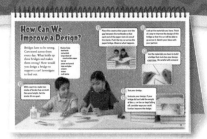

Name _____

Essential Question

How Can We Improve a Design?

Set a Purpose
What will you discover in this activity?

_____

_____

Think About the Procedure
How could you and your partner redesign the bridge to make it stronger?

_____

_____

_____

_____

Do you and your partner have different ideas for changing the bridge? Explain.

_____

_____

_____

_____

Record Your Data
Sketch your idea for a new bridge design. Make notes about how it differs from the first bridge.

81

Draw Conclusions

What were the best features of your design? What were the worst features? Explain.

_____

_____

_____

_____

_____

Analyze and Extend

1. Look at the bridges that other students made. What did all the new bridges that worked have in common?

_____

_____

_____

_____

2. What were the main reasons that the first bridge collapsed?

_____

_____

_____

_____

3. How could looking at the design of other bridges help you redesign your own bridge?

_____

_____

_____

_____

_____

4. What other questions do you have about how things can be redesigned?

_____

_____

_____

_____

DETOUR

1

Civil engineers plan the structures that are built in cities and towns. Roads and bridges are some of the things they plan.

2

The projects that civil engineers build need to be safe. They must hold up to daily use.

3

Civil engineers improve how we live. They help people get the things they need.

4

Civil engineers are important to a growing city or town. They look at the need for new structures.

8 Things YOU SHOULD KNOW ABOUT Civil Engineers

5

Civil engineers keep cars and trucks moving. They fix roads that are no longer safe.

6

Civil engineers make drawings called construction plans.

7

Civil engineers use tools, such as compasses and rulers. Many engineers use computers.

8

Some civil engineers measure the surface of the land. They use this data to plan buildings.

Engineering Emergency!

Match the problems that can be solved by a civil engineer with its solution in the illustration. Write the number of the problem in the correct triangle on the picture.

1 We have an energy shortage! We can harness the river's energy to generate electricity.

2 The city is getting crowded! More people are moving here. They need more places to live and work.

3 The streets are always jammed. We have a transportation crisis!

4 The nearest bridge is too far away. We need a faster and easier way to get across the river.

Think About It!

If you were a civil engineer, what kind of changes would you make where you live?

_____

_____

Unit 2 Review

Vocabulary Review

Use the terms in the box to complete the sentences.

> design process
> technology

1. When Ms. Simm's third graders designed a tunnel, they followed steps in a _____.

2. A dishwasher is an example of something that makes a family's life easier and is a kind of _____.

Science Concepts

Fill in the letter of the choice that best answers the question.

3. The Johnson family decided to purchase a new vehicle. An important feature they searched for is four-wheel drive, because four-wheel drive works well in snow. Why is the invention of four-wheel drive a kind of technology?

    Ⓐ It solves the problem of increasing vehicle size.

    Ⓑ It meets the needs of drivers.

    Ⓒ It protects the environment.

    Ⓓ It decreases safety.

4. Stewart will be working with a team to design an improved outdoor light. What should they do before beginning improvements?

    Ⓐ improve their new design

    Ⓑ keep the old design just as it is

    Ⓒ test their new design

    Ⓓ test the old design

5. What is the **main** goal of the design process?

    Ⓐ to find solutions to problems

    Ⓑ to give scientists something to do

    Ⓒ to make charts and graphs

    Ⓓ to write articles for magazines

6. Grace, Miguel, and Amelia are studying how improving technologies can affect the environment. They have to design an invention that affects the environment in a positive way. Which invention do you think they picked?

    Ⓐ a bus that uses more gas than others

    Ⓑ a car tire that cannot be recycled

    Ⓒ an electric train that does not run on fuel

    Ⓓ a new fabric made from rare plants

Science Concepts

Fill in the letter of the choice that best answers the question.

7. Grocery stores can be very busy places. After people fill up their carts with what they need, they may have to stand in line for a while. The inventor of self-checkout lanes improved technology to help consumers. What new needs could self-checkout lanes cause?

Ⓐ colder freezer and refrigerator sections

Ⓑ automatic-bagging technology

Ⓒ safer pesticide use on produce

Ⓓ improved travel technology

8. Kelsey is researching new computers. She wants to find the computer with the newest technology. Which computer is she most likely to choose?

Ⓐ the biggest computer

Ⓑ the least expensive computer

Ⓒ the oldest computer

Ⓓ the computer with the fastest processing speed

9. What problem did adding air conditioning to cars solve?

Ⓐ Car engines got too hot during the summer.

Ⓑ People got too cold inside cars during the winter.

Ⓒ People got too hot inside cars during the summer.

Ⓓ The car radio got too hot during the hot summer days.

10. This is a technology that helped John's grandmother.

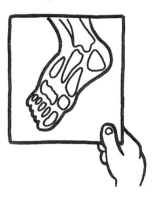

How did this technology most likely help John's grandmother?

Ⓐ It showed his grandmother that she was wearing the wrong size shoe.

Ⓑ It showed his grandmother what type of socks she should wear.

Ⓒ It showed that his grandmother's foot did not have bones.

Ⓓ It showed his grandmother's broken bones.

11. Scientists notice a problem with an engine. It is getting too hot after it runs for a long time. What should the scientists do **next**?

Ⓐ take the engine apart

Ⓑ plan and build a new engine

Ⓒ test and improve the new engine design

Ⓓ communicate results of the new engine design

12. An engineer designs a new engine, but one of the parts keeps melting. The engine can get hotter than 240 °C. Look at the table.

Material	Melting Point (°C)
potassium	64
plastic	120
tin	232
aluminum	660

Which material would you suggest the engineer use in the next design?

Ⓐ aluminum

Ⓑ plastic

Ⓒ potassium

Ⓓ tin

13. Suppose you are digging a stone out of the ground with a shovel. You have a problem after you dig all the dirt around the stone. The stone is too heavy to lift. What is your **best** option in solving this problem?

Ⓐ continue to try lifting it yourself

Ⓑ start over and pick a smaller rock

Ⓒ use a bigger shovel

Ⓓ use a tractor to pull it out of the ground

14. Suppose you are in a tree house you built. You notice that one of the boards is broken and could cause an accident. How could you improve your design?

Ⓐ paint the board with a bright color

Ⓑ replace the board with stronger wood

Ⓒ replace the entire floor

Ⓓ tear down the tree house

15. The chart below shows the number of miles per gallon of gas used by some cars. The cars that use the least gas travel more miles per gallon. How many cars use the least amount of gas?

Gas Mileage Per Gallon of Gasoline

Miles Per Gallon	Tally of Car Models
9–12	I
13–16	III
17– 20	IIII
21–25	III
26–30	IIIII
31–34	IIIIIIII
35–40	II

Each tally mark represents 1 model car.

Ⓐ 1

Ⓑ 2

Ⓒ 7

Ⓓ 9

Apply Inquiry and Review the Big Idea

Write the answers to these questions.

Use the picture to answer question 16.

16. Write three kinds of technology shown in the scene and describe how each improves society.

_____

_____

_____

17. You move to a new home with a doghouse in the backyard. Your small dog cannot get into the doghouse easily because it is raised up off the ground.

What is the problem? What can you do to solve this problem?

_____

_____

_____

Rocks and Soil

© Houghton Mifflin Harcourt Publishing Company   (border) ©NDisc/age fotostock; (bg) ©Kevin Fleming/Corbis VCG/Getty Images; (inset) ©Natalia Kuzmina/Alamy

Big Idea

Rocks and soil have characteristics that are used to classify and describe them. Water and wind change rocks and soil over time.

S3E1, S3E1.a, S3E1.b, S3E1.c

Stone Mountain, Georgia

I Wonder Why

Why do trees grow all around the mountain but not on its sides? *Turn the page to find out.*

Here's Why Soil is made up of many components which allow plants to grow in it. Water and wind change rock to help form soil.

In this unit, you will explore the Big Idea, the Essential Questions, and the Investigations on the Inquiry Flipchart.

Levels of Inquiry Key ■ DIRECTED ■ GUIDED ■ INDEPENDENT

Track Your Progress

Big Idea Rocks and soil have characteristics that are used to classify and describe them. Water and wind change rocks and soil over time.

Essential Questions

Now I Get the Big Idea!

Science Notebook

Before you begin each lesson, be sure to write your thoughts about the Essential Question.

© Houghton Mifflin Harcourt Publishing Company (border) ©Nbber/Age Fotostock (c) ©Kevin Fleming/Corbis.V/loc/Getty Images (inset) ©Natalie Kuzmina/Alamy

Essential Question

What Are Characteristics of Rocks?

Engage Your Brain!

Find the answer to the following question in this lesson and record it here.

Rocks come in many colors. What causes the different colors of rocks?

_____

_____

_____

Active Reading

Lesson Vocabulary

List the term. As you learn about the term, make notes in the Interactive Glossary.

_____

_____

_____

Signal Words: Details

Signal words show connections between ideas. *For example* signals examples of an idea. *Also* signals added facts. Active readers remember what they read because they are alert to signal words that identify examples and facts about a topic.

What Is Your Favorite Color?

Have you ever picked up a rock because of its color?

Active Reading As you read these two pages, circle signal words that identify examples and added facts.

One of the first things you might notice about a rock is its color. The colors of rocks are caused by the different minerals that make them up. A **mineral** [MIN•er•uhl] is any nonliving solid that has a crystal form. For example, granite can appear grey, black, or pink depending on the amounts of different minerals in the rock.

Each of these rocks is granite even though each has a different color.

Like granite, many rocks have more than one color. That's because they are made up of more than one kind of mineral. Rocks can also appear blue, brown, red, orange, green, and white.

▶ Artists can make colorful patterns and designs using rocks. List four colors of rocks that you see in the rock design on these two pages.

_____

_____

_____

_____

Do the Math!
Find the Total

An artist has 36 red rocks, 22 blue rocks, and 64 white rocks to make a United States flag. How many rocks does she have in all?

_____

Telling the Texture

Have you ever used sandpaper? Like rocks, different textures of sandpaper have different-sized grains.

Active Reading As you read, underline the sentence that tells what makes up the texture of a rock.

The surface of sandpaper is covered with small, rough grains. Some sandpaper has grains that are big and have sharp edges. Other sandpaper has grains that are small and smoother. A rock's texture depends on the shape and size of the small grains that make up the rock.

coarse-grained

Rocks that have large grains or crystals are coarse-grained. Most of the rock is made up of rice-sized grains or larger.

conglomerate

gabbro

You can clearly see the pebbles and crystals in these coarse-grained rocks.

medium-grained

You can still see the grains in medium-grained rocks. But the grains are smaller than in coarse-grained rocks.

sandstone

This piece of sandstone is medium-grained.

fine-grained

If the grains are so small that you need a hand lens to see them, the rock is fine-grained.

siltstone

Fine-grained rocks have tiny grains.

▶ Classify each rock based on its texture.

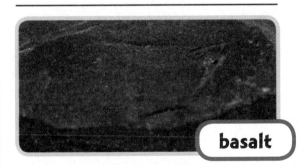

basalt

pegmatite

Ooh, Shiny!

Imagine hiking along a riverbed. You see a bright flash among the rocks. When you look closer, you see a shiny rock among the many dull ones on the river's bottom. What makes it shiny?

Active Reading On this page, underline two words that describe luster.

Another property used to classify rocks is luster. *Luster* describes how a material reflects light. Luster can be described using words such as *metallic* and *nonmetallic*.

metallic luster

The shiny rock in the riverbed might be a gold nugget! Copper, gold, and silver each have a metallic luster. Rocks that have a metallic luster have the look of polished metal. A rock with a metallic luster looks shiny because light reflects well off its surface.

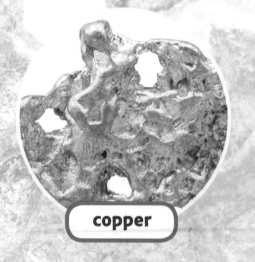

copper

gold

nonmetallic luster

A rock that does not look like polished metal at all has a nonmetallic luster. Many rocks have nonmetallic luster. To classify rocks better, scientists describe different kinds of nonmetallic luster. For example some rocks, such as quartz, reflect light like glass. They have a glassy luster. Other rocks, like gypsum [JIP▪suhm], do not reflect light well and look very plain. These rocks have a dull luster.

quartz

gypsum

▶ This rock is found near old or active volcanoes. How would you classify it based on luster?

_____

How Hard Is It?

A dry, stale roll might be "as hard as a rock." But how hard IS a rock?

Active Reading On this page, circle the photos of rocks that you can scratch with your fingernail.

Hardness is one characteristic used to classify rocks. You test hardness by trying to scratch the rock. In 1812, a scientist named Friedrich Mohs [mohz] developed a scale to compare hardnesses.

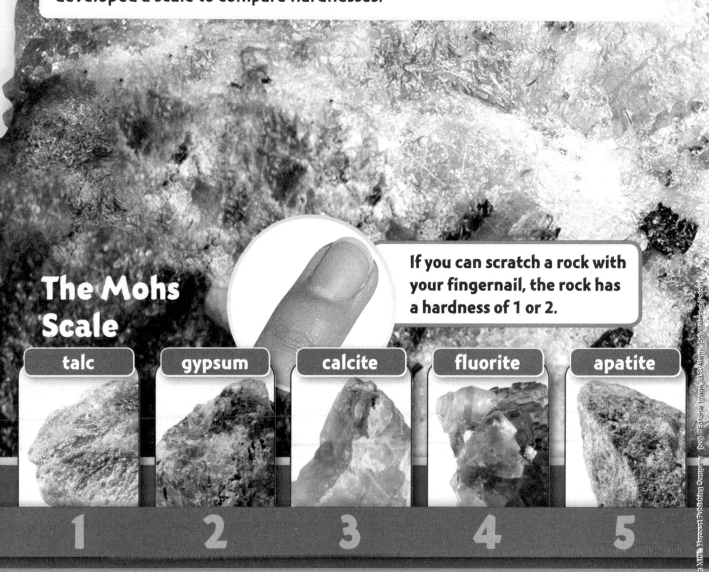

The Mohs Scale

If you can scratch a rock with your fingernail, the rock has a hardness of 1 or 2.

talc	gypsum	calcite	fluorite	apatite
1	2	3	4	5

On the Mohs scale, a mineral with a higher number can scratch rocks with a lower or equal number. The softest rocks score a 1. Every other mineral can scratch rocks with a hardness of 1. The hardest mineral—a diamond—scores a 10 on the Mohs scale. A diamond can't be scratched by any mineral except another diamond.

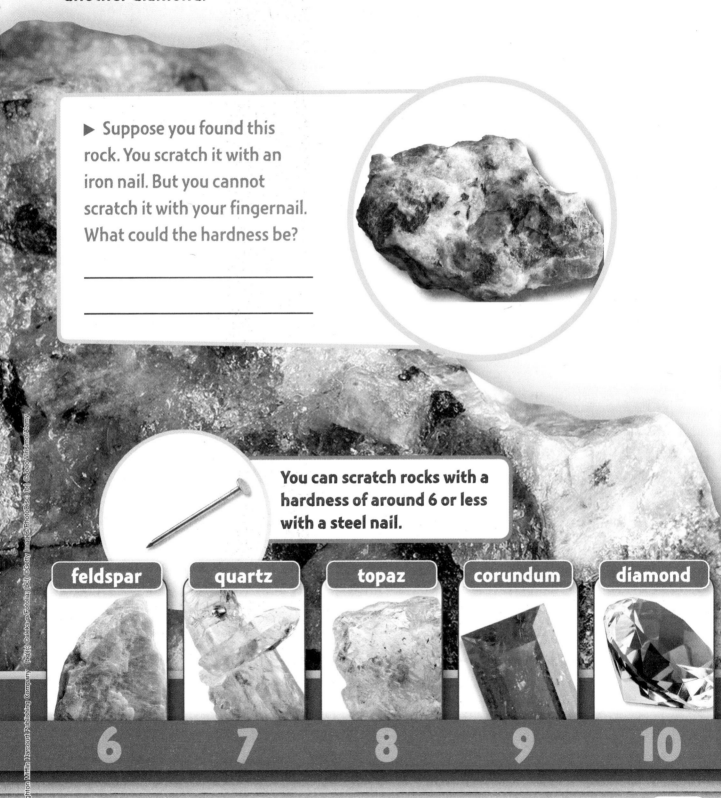

▶ Suppose you found this rock. You scratch it with an iron nail. But you cannot scratch it with your fingernail. What could the hardness be?

_____

_____

You can scratch rocks with a hardness of around 6 or less with a steel nail.

feldspar	quartz	topaz	corundum	diamond
6	7	8	9	10

Sum It Up!

When you're done, use the answer key to check and revise your work.

Change the circled part of each statement to make it correct.

1

Rocks that shine like metals have a metallic (texture.)

_____

2

Rocks that are made up of very small grains are (coarse-grained.)

_____

3

A rock that can be scratched by a steel nail has a hardness of around (4 or greater.)

_____

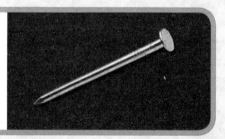

4

A (rock) is any nonliving solid that has a crystal form.

_____

5

An artist that wants to make a necklace and matching earrings of polished rocks would likely look for rocks that have the same (hardness.)

_____

© Houghton Mifflin Harcourt Publishing Company (1) ©michal812/Fotolia; (2) ©www.sandatlas.org/Shutterstock; (3) ©Getty Images/PhotoDisc; (4) ©Carlosdelacalle/iStock/Getty Images; (5) ©Natalia/Fotolia

Brain Check

Name _____

Word Play

1

Unscramble the letters to complete each clue.	
1. How a rock reflects light is a characteristic called _____.	stelur
2. You might use a hand lens to help classify rocks by their _____.	truexet
3. You can test a rock's _____ using your fingernail and a steel nail.	redshans
4. A rock that is made up of large crystals has a _____-grained texture.	sorcea
5. A rock that is very shiny is classified as having a _____ luster.	leltimac

Apply Concepts

2 Identify the color, texture, and luster of the rocks shown.

Color: _____   Color: _____

Texture: _____   Texture: _____

Luster: _____   Luster: _____

3 Describe how you test a rock for hardness.

_____

_____

_____

_____

_____

Take It Home! Collect rocks from your neighborhood or park. Make a label for each that describes its characteristics. Show them to a friend or family member.

Name _____

Essential Question

How Can We Classify Rocks?

Set a Purpose
What will you learn from this experiment?

_____

_____

_____

Think About the Procedure

1. Do you expect each group to classify the rocks in the same way? State your prediction.

_____

_____

_____

_____

2. What tools are available and why?

_____

_____

_____

Record Your Results
In the space below, make a table to record your observations of the rock samples.

Draw Conclusions

Classify your rocks and explain the basis of your classification.

_____

_____

_____

_____

_____

_____

Analyze and Extend

1. Describe a different way to classify your rocks.

_____

_____

_____

_____

_____

_____

2. How would working with all the minerals on the Mohs scale affect your results?

_____

_____

_____

_____

_____

3. What other questions do you have about classifying rocks?

_____

_____

_____

_____

_____

_____

Essential Question

What Is Soil?

Engage Your Brain!

Find the answer to the following question in this lesson and record it here.

Why is soil important to these peach trees and to people?

_____

_____

_____

Active Reading

Lesson Vocabulary

List the terms. As you learn about each one, make notes in the Interactive Glossary.

_____ _____

_____ _____

_____ _____

Compare and Contrast

Many ideas in this lesson are connected because they explain comparisons and contrasts—how things are alike and different. Active readers stay focused on comparisons and contrasts when they ask themselves, How are things alike? How are they different?

Soil Is Not Just Dirt

Soil is important. Why? Most plants need soil to grow. Without plants, there would be no food for animals or people.

Active Reading As you read these two pages, draw a star next to what you think is the most important sentence. Be ready to explain why you think so.

When you are in a forest or garden, or even a parking lot, what is under your feet? Below the sticks, rocks, plants, and pavement, there is soil. **Soil** is a mixture of water, air, tiny pieces of rock, and humus. **Humus** is a rich mixture of the decomposed, or broken down, remains of plants and animals.

There are many kinds of soil. Soil can be black, red, brown, gray, and even white. Soil can be moist or dry. It can contain different kinds of minerals—even gold!

Soil is a mixture of decomposing plants and animals, small bits of rock, air, and water.

Some kinds of soil are better for growing plants than other kinds. Soil that is very good for plants is *fertile*. It can take hundreds or even thousands of years to form. Because soil is such an important natural resource, it must be conserved.

The dead leaves on this forest floor will decompose and become part of the soil.

Farmers must take care of the soil so it will remain fertile.

Soil Is a Natural Resource

Why is soil important to people and animals?

_____

_____

_____

_____

_____

How Does Soil Form?

If you dig deep into the soil, you can see that soil has different layers.

As you read these two pages, draw one line under a cause. Draw two lines under the effect.

The top layer of soil is called *topsoil*. It is the most fertile soil layer. Plants grow in the topsoil. Topsoil is fertile because it contains humus. Humus makes the soil darker.

The layer beneath topsoil is called *subsoil*. Subsoil does not have a lot of humus, but it does have small pieces of rock. If you dig deep enough into the soil, you will reach solid rock. This is *bedrock.*

How does soil form? It forms from bedrock. When bedrock is at Earth's surface, it breaks down by weathering. Rain, wind, and other things weather bedrock, so big pieces of rock get smaller and smaller. Eventually, bedrock is broken into small bits of rock. These mix with air, water, and humus to form soil.

Soil Layers

Bedrock is solid rock. The small pieces of rock in the upper layers of soil come from bedrock.

Surface litter such as leaves, sticks, and rocks lies on top of soil. Plants and animals can be found above the soil and inside the soil, too.

Topsoil is the layer of soil closest to Earth's surface. Topsoil is where most plants grow. Topsoil is fertile because it contains humus. It also contains small bits of weathered bedrock.

Subsoil is one or more layers of soil that lie between the topsoil and bedrock. Subsoil contains slightly larger pieces of rock than topsoil and little or no humus.

Describe the Layers

Complete the chart by describing each layer of soil.

Topsoil	
Subsoil	
Bedrock	

Types of Soil

There are more than 70,000 kinds of soil in the United States alone! What makes them different from one another?

Active Reading As you read these two pages, draw boxes around the names of things that are being contrasted.

As you know, soil contains humus as well as water, air, and bits of rock. One way to distinguish among soils is by the sizes of their particles.

Tiny particles of rock that you can see with just your eyes are called **sand**. **Silt** is tiny particles of rock that are difficult to see with only your eyes. Particles of rock that are even smaller than silt are called **clay**.

The amounts of sand, silt, and clay in soil give it texture. Texture is how the soil feels in your hands. Soil with more sand feels rough, while soil with more clay feels smooth. Soils can be made up of different minerals, depending on the area where the soils formed. A soil's color also depends on where it formed.

Most soils contain all three kinds of soil particles.

Soils that contain a lot of clay particles are fertile but heavy and sticky. They hold moisture well. They get very cold in winter, but dry out and get hard in the summer.

Sandy soils let water pass through easily. They dry out quickly. Sandy soils are usually light and easy to dig.

Soils that are mostly silt feel slippery when they are wet. They hold moisture for a long time. They also hold nutrients very well.

▶ Why does water pass through sandy soils more quickly than through soils that contain mostly clay or silt?

_____

_____

Plants Need Soil

What do plants get from soil? They get nutrients, water, and a place to live.

Active Reading As you read these two pages, find and underline the definition of *nutrients*.

Plants need water and light to grow. They also need nutrients. **Nutrients** are substances that plants take in from the soil through their roots to help them live and grow.

The best kind of soil for most plants is called *loam*. Loam has a balance of silt, sand, and clay. It is rich in nutrients and humus, it stays moist, and it is easy to dig. Some plants, though, grow better in other types of soil.

Plants take in nutrients and water from the soil through their roots.

Cabbage grows well in clay soils.

Sea grapes and sea oats grow on sandy beaches.

Which Soil Matches the Plant?

Look at the images above. What can you conclude about the soil requirements of these plants?

_____

_____

In which of these soils do most types of cactus grow? What does this tell you about cactuses?

_____

_____

Composting

Don't throw away that banana peel! You can use fruit peels and other kitchen scraps to help plants grow.

Active Reading As you read these two pages, find and underline two facts about compost.

Compost is humus that you make yourself. Pile plant parts, such as dried leaves and grass, into a big container. Then add scraps of fruits and vegetables. Tiny organisms too small to see will decompose the scraps to make humus. Spread compost on your plants so they will grow quickly and stay healthy.

Compost does more than help plants in your garden. Making compost means that you don't throw away as much garbage. When people throw away less garbage, that's good for everyone!

Add things like eggshells, peelings, and fruits and vegetables to compost. You can even add newspaper. Don't add animal products such as meat and cheese.

Do the Math!
Use Subtraction

It can take 850 years for 2 cm of soil to form. It can take 6 months to make 2 cm of compost for your garden. How much longer does it take soil to form than it does to make compost?

_____

_____

Sum It Up!

When you're done, use the answer key to check
and revise your work.

**The blue words in each summary statement are incorrect.
Write words to replace the blue parts.**

1
Compost is material
that helps plants grow
because it contains a lot of clay.

_____

2
Soil is made quickly
in nature.

_____

3
Plants need soil for
support and light.

_____

4
Weathering causes
humus below the soil to
break into smaller pieces.

_____

5
Silty soil contains the
largest particles of rock.

_____

6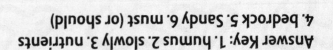
Topsoil is so important to plant
growth around the world that
people do not need to conserve it.

_____

Answer Key: 1. humus 2. slowly 3. nutrients
4. bedrock 5. Sandy 6. must (or should)

Brain Check

Name _____

Word Play

1 **Use the words in the box to complete the puzzle.**

soil*	humus*	sand*	silt*	clay*	nutrients*
bedrock	loam	compost	plants	*Key Lesson Vocabulary	

Across

1. The type of soil that drains water most quickly _____
3. Living things that need soil for support _____
5. The type of soil that holds water for the longest time _____
6. The type of soil that has tiny particles of rock bigger than clay but smaller than sand _____
7. This is weathered by wind and water to make soil. _____
8. Something found in soil that is made of dead plants and animals _____

Down

1. This provides plants with the water and nutrients they need to survive. _____
2. This is the best kind of soil for plants. It is made of the three soil types. _____
4. Substances in soil that plants need to grow _____
5. Can be made using kitchen scraps and dead plants _____

117

Apply Concepts

2 Answer the questions about the picture.

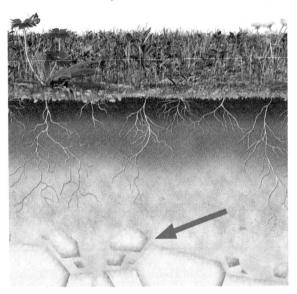

Explain why you can see darker soil toward the top of the soil layers.

_____

_____

_____

_____

What is happening where the red arrow is pointing?

_____

_____

3 Fill in the blanks to make the statements true.

When bedrock breaks down for a long time and mixes with air, water, and the decomposed remains of _____ , soil is formed. Soil is a resource because plants need it to _____ , and we depend on plants for our _____ . Soil supports plants and gives them the _____ they need to grow.

Take It Home!

With an adult, look at the soil in your yard or at a park. Which type of soil is it? Is it a mixture? Write down your observations and share them with the class.

Meet the Environmental Scientists

Noah Idechong

Noah Idechong grew up in a small fishing village on the island nation of Palau. Palauan children are taught to take special care of the ocean. The ocean provides their families with food. Idechong worked to conserve ocean life. Boats can damage coral on the coast. When the coral dies, many fish leave, and the fish populations get smaller. Idechong helped make rules to protect the coastal environment.

Many kinds of fish swim in island waters. By putting limits on fishing in certain areas, more fish can survive and reproduce.

This scientist is measuring a soil property called pH. Different types of plants grow best at different pH ranges. This property is important for brake ferns, because it can affect the amount of arsenic these plants can take in.

Lena Qiying Ma

Lena Qiying Ma was a soil scientist. She studied how some plants take in arsenic [AR•suh•nik]. Arsenic is used as a poison to keep weeds away from crops. During her research, Ma found a fern growing in an industrial site. It was green even though the soil was polluted with arsenic. Ma discovered that ferns remove arsenic from soil. She studied how the fern can be used to clean up pollution in soil and groundwater.

Be a Soil Scientist!

A farmer is planting his crops. He tests the pH of the soil from different fields on his farm. He wants to know which crop to plant in each field.

Broccoli grows best in soil that has a pH around 6.

Sugar beets grow best in soil that has a pH around 8.

Blueberries grow best in soil that has a pH around 4.

Use the pH scale below to match the soil from each field with the best crop to plant in that field. Write the name of the crop on the line for the correct soil.

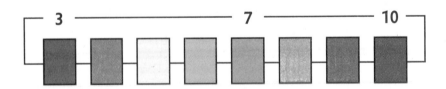

3 ——————— 7 ——————— 10

_____   _____   _____

Essential Question

How Does Earth's Surface Change Slowly?

Engage Your Brain!

Find the answer to the following question in this lesson and record it here.

This glacier is moving slowly. How is it affecting the land around it?

_____

_____

_____

Active Reading

Lesson Vocabulary

List the terms. As you read, make notes about them in the Interactive Glossary.

_____ _____

_____

Signal Words: Main Idea

Words that signal a main idea include *most important* and *in general.* Active readers remember what they read because they are alert to signal words that identify important ideas.

What Weathering Can Do

Animals, plants, water, and temperature are just some of the things that can change Earth's surface.

Active Reading As you read these two pages, underline details about what water does to change Earth's surface.

Weathering is the breaking down of rock into smaller pieces. This can happen when tree roots push into the surface of rock. It can happen when animals burrow into the ground.

Weathering is often caused by patterns of freezing and thawing. As winter nears, the weather gets colder. Rain falls into cracks in rock and freezes. As liquid water turns to ice, it expands. This widens the cracks. When the ice melts, or thaws, the rock is weaker. Pieces crumble and fall away. Little by little, the shape of the rock changes. Smaller pieces of rock may become part of the soil.

Change Takes Time

Changing seasons cause patterns of freezing and thawing. This is one way weathering happens.

Water moves into cracks and stays there.

Weathering by water has caused these rocks to become rounded. Freezing water has also caused some of the rocks to crack.

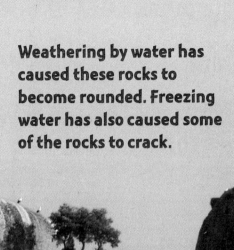

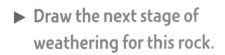
▶ Draw the next stage of weathering for this rock.

①

②

③

The water freezes. Ice forms in the cracks. The ice takes up more space than the liquid water did.

The ice widens the cracks. Pieces of rock may break off.

Erosion Motion

Water, wind, and glaciers never stop moving. They carry soil, rocks, and sand along with them. Over time, this movement changes the shape of the land.

Active Reading As you read, circle a word or a phrase that signals a main idea.

In general, **erosion** happens when soil, rocks, or sand are moved. Wind, water, and glaciers can all cause erosion. It happens everywhere. When waves at a beach wash away sand, that's erosion. When wind blows sand in a desert, that's erosion. When rainfall carries mud into a river, that's erosion.

Glaciers are another cause of erosion. A **glacier** is a large, thick sheet of moving ice. Glaciers slide along slowly. As they move, many glaciers cut paths through the ground. They pick up pieces of weathered rock, sand, and soil. Glaciers push or carry the rocks and soil as they move. Sometimes glaciers move enough soil to form a whole island!

Wind and waves cause weathering as they hit the rock. This breaks the rock into smaller pieces.

Wind and water move sand. This erosion causes one part of the beach to become smaller. Another part of the beach becomes larger when the eroded sand is left there.

Over time, erosion can cause big changes. It has caused this beach to become much smaller than it once was.

When this lighthouse was built, it was far from the cliff's edge. But wind and waves have weathered and eroded the cliff. Now, the lighthouse must be moved to a safer spot.

Do the Math!
Solve a Word Problem

A lighthouse is 60 meters from the edge of a cliff. The cliff erodes by 3 meters each year. How long will it take for the edge of the cliff to reach the lighthouse? Show your work.

_____

Sand, soil, and small rocks erode away. The eroded material moves into the water and away from the land.

Soil Moves Around

Erosion can ruin fields and forests by taking away soil the plants need. But soil that is washed away from one place can help plants in another place.

Active Reading As you read, underline the harmful and helpful effects of erosion.

As a river flows between its banks, soil and rocks are swept along. The water carries them downstream. Now, there is less soil on the riverbanks. Tree roots may be uncovered. Plants that need the soil may be affected. Without the support of their roots anchored in deep soil, the trees may fall.

But soil that is washed away from a riverbank ends up somewhere else. As a river nears the ocean, the water moves more slowly. The rocks and soil in the river are dropped. This process makes a landform called a *delta*. A river delta is full of rich soil.

Water has eroded soil from this riverbank. These trees may soon fall.

The river's motion carries soil downstream. This leaves less soil for the plants that are growing here.

As a river nears the ocean, the water slows. Soil and rocks in the river are left behind.

Over time, the rocks and soil form a delta. The rich soil of a river delta is a great place for plants to grow.

Cause and Effect

Fill in the blanks to tell the causes and effects of erosion.

1. Moving water carries rocks and _____ downstream.

2. Growing _____ along the riverbanks may become loose.

3. Tree _____ may be uncovered, causing the trees to fall.

4. The rocks and soil may be deposited, forming a _____.

Sum It Up!

When you're done, use the answer key to check and revise your work.

Fill in the missing words in the summary. Then complete the cause-and-effect graphic organizer.

Summarize

Weathering and erosion are two processes that (1) ________________ the shape of Earth's surface. When large pieces of rock are broken down into smaller pieces, it is called (2) ________________. Erosion is when (3) ________________, wind, or glaciers carry these smaller rocks to new places. Erosion can change beaches and riverbanks by taking sand and (4) ________________ away. But it can also make new landforms, such as river (5) ________________.

Cause		Effect
Waves crash against a cliff.	→	6. ________________
7. ________________	→	A lighthouse needs to be moved.

1. change 2. weathering 3. water 4. soil 5. deltas 6. The waves weather and erode the cliff. 7. The land gets smaller every year.

Name _____

Word Play

1 Use the words in the box at the bottom of the page to complete the puzzle.

Across

2. A river carries soil here
4. To melt after freezing
5. This part of a plant can cause weathering.
8. When wind and water move rocks, sand, or soil
9. A large, moving sheet of ice
10. When a solid turns to a liquid

Down

1. Breaking of rock into smaller pieces
3. Another word for stones
6. Change from a liquid to a solid
7. When this is washed away, plants cannot grow.

rocks	delta
thaw	weathering*
glacier*	root
melt	erosion*
soil	freeze

* Key Lesson Vocabulary

Apply Concepts

2 For each picture, draw how the object in the picture would change.

 **+** time **+** waves **=**

 **+** time **+** rain **=**

 **+** time **+** rushing river **=**

3 Name two things that can happen when soil is eroded by a river.

_____

_____

_____

Take It Home!

With your family, talk about weathering and erosion. Observe soil or rock in your neighborhood that has changed over time and explain how water or wind caused the changes.

Sand and Surf:
Erosion Technology

There is often more than one solution to an engineering problem. To choose the best solution, people make trade-offs. A trade-off is giving up one feature to make another feature better. Read about the trade-offs of two beach erosion solutions.

People can control beach erosion by building a jetty. A jetty begins on a beach and runs into the water. It is at a right angle to the shore.

Jetty Pluses	Jetty Minuses
Easier to build above water	Erodes beach on other side of jetty
Can be built quickly	Changes the natural look of the beach

People can control beach erosion by building a reef. A reef is under water. It runs in the same direction as the shore.

Reef Pluses	Reef Minuses
Does not erode nearby beaches	Harder to build under water
Lowers wave energy before it reaches beach	Takes time for the reef to form

continued

Analyze Trade-offs

Below are two solutions for soil erosion. Fill in the charts to show the trade-offs. Then tell which you would choose and why.

Hay Bales Pluses	Hay Bales Minuses

Silt Fence Pluses	Silt Fence Minuses

Hay bales are made of packed dry grass. They are large and heavy. They are put on top of the ground.

A silt fence is made of lightweight plastic. The bottom is dug into the ground.

Which soil erosion solution would you choose? Why?

_____

_____

Build On It!

Rise to the engineering design challenge—complete **Improvise It: Reducing Erosion** on the Inquiry Flipchart.

Name _____

Essential Question

How Can We Model Erosion?

Set a Purpose
What will you learn from this modeling activity?

_____

_____

_____

Think About the Procedure
What does the sand represent? What does the ice cube represent?

_____

_____

_____

_____

Why will you push the ice over clay before you push it over the sand and clay?

_____

_____

_____

Record Your Observations
Use words or drawings to show how the ice and sand interact.

	Sight	Touch
Clay Without Sand		
Clay With Sand		

Draw Conclusions

How does a glacier affect the land it moves over?

_____

_____

_____

_____

Analyze and Extend

1. What force causes a glacier to move downhill?

_____

_____

_____

2. You pushed the ice over the clay and soil to see the effects of a glacier. In nature, glaciers travel much more slowly. How could you model the way that glaciers move in nature?

_____

_____

_____

3. As glaciers move down a slope to the sea, do they cause weathering, erosion, or both? Explain your answer.

_____

_____

_____

_____

_____

_____

4. What are some other questions you have about glaciers and how glaciers affect the land?

_____

_____

_____

_____

_____

_____

Name _____

Vocabulary Review

Use the terms in the box to complete the sentences.

| humus |
| minerals |
| nutrients |
| soil |
| weathering |

1. A part of soil with a rich mixture of decomposing plants and animals is _____.

2. A rock breaks apart after freezing and thawing many times. This is an example of _____.

3. A mixture of minerals, air, water, and humus is _____.

4. Quartz is one of many _____ because it is a nonliving solid with a crystal form.

5. To grow, plants need water, light, and _____ from the soil.

Science Concepts

Fill in the letter of the choice that best answers the question.

6. How can glaciers cause erosion?

   Ⓐ They can push together Earth's surface, making mountains.

   Ⓑ They can cause vibrations that crack Earth's crust.

   Ⓒ They can fill cracks in rocks that get larger and break the rocks.

   Ⓓ They can pick up bits of rock and soil and carry them as they move.

7. Sonya sorts her rock collection into categories labeled nonmetallic and metallic. What characteristic did she use to classify the rocks?

   Ⓐ texture

   Ⓑ luster

   Ⓒ hardness

   Ⓓ color

Science Concepts

Fill in the letter of the choice that best answers the question.

8. Hector wants to put some soil in a pot that will drain water quickly. Which soil particle should be the largest part of the soil?

  Ⓐ clay

  Ⓑ humus

  Ⓒ sand

  Ⓓ silt

9. Which describes how water can cause weathering?

  Ⓐ Rivers flow through a canyon. As they move, they carry rocks with them, making the canyon steeper.

  Ⓑ Glaciers are made of ice. As they move, they pick up pieces of soil and rock and move the soil and rock along with them.

  Ⓒ Water flows into cracks in rocks. The water freezes, making the cracks larger and breaking down the rock.

  Ⓓ Rain falls quickly during a storm. This causes the mud on a hill to move and large areas of dirt and rock to slide down a hill.

10. Tyrone wants to make sure his soil is mostly clay particles. What should he look for?

  Ⓐ The soil will dry out quickly.

  Ⓑ The soil will be heavy and sticky.

  Ⓒ The soil will feel slippery when wet.

  Ⓓ The soil will have small particles that he can see.

11. Tran's class is visiting a delta to make observations. The students observe rich soil. What is the most likely reason for this?

  Ⓐ Rocks in the delta were ground into soil.

  Ⓑ The soil was carried into the delta by the wind.

  Ⓒ The soil was washed into the delta by a flowing river.

  Ⓓ Rocks from the ocean were ground up by ocean waves.

12. Keesha puts some brick pieces, sand, and water in a jar. She shakes it each day for two weeks and notices what happens to the brick pieces and water. What is she modeling?

Ⓐ how rocks are classified

Ⓑ how weathering forms soil

Ⓒ how soil provides nutrients to plants

Ⓓ how to determine hardness of rocks

13. Giorgio made the soil model below.

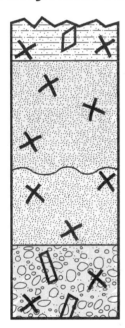

Which names the top layer in his drawing?

Ⓐ bedrock

Ⓑ silt

Ⓒ subsoil

Ⓓ topsoil

14. Why is loam the best kind of soil for plants?

Ⓐ It is rich in nutrients to help the plants grow.

Ⓑ It is heavy and thick, so it supports the plants.

Ⓒ It has the most sand, so water drains quickly.

Ⓓ It has more air pockets, so it allows light to reach the roots.

15. Lucinda classifies her rocks by hardness. She tests a new rock using her fingernail, a steel nail, and a crystal of fluorite. The steel nail scratches the rock. The rock is not scratched by her fingernail or the fluorite. In which group should Lucinda place the new rock?

Ⓐ hardness 1 to 2

Ⓑ hardness 3 to 4

Ⓒ hardness 5 to 6

Ⓓ hardness 6 to 10

Apply Inquiry and Review the Big Idea

Write the answers to these questions.

16. Look at the drawing below.

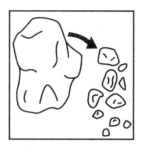

What process is shown in this drawing? How can soil form from this process?

_____

_____

_____

17. Ahmed observes five rocks. He records the data in the table.

Rock	Characteristics
1	blue, coarse-grained, dull
2	red, medium-grained, dull
3	blue, fine-grained, glassy
4	silver, fine-grained, metallic
5	red, fine-grained, glassy

Ahmed classifies the rocks in three groups: rocks 1 and 3, rocks 2 and 5, and rock 4. Analyze the data. What characteristic did he use? What is another way to classify the rocks?

_____

_____

_____

Fossils

Big Idea

Fossils help us understand Earth's history.

S3E2., S3E2.a, S3E2.b

I Wonder Why

These are shellfish fossils. Animals like these live in the ocean. Why were these fossils found on mountaintops? *Turn the page to find out.*

Here's Why Fossils can tell scientists about past environments. Ocean, or marine, fossils found on mountaintops indicate that the area was once covered by an ocean. Over time the land changed, and the layers that contained the fossils rose above sea level.

In this unit, you will explore the Big Idea, the Essential Questions, and the Investigations on the Inquiry Flipchart.

Levels of Inquiry Key ■ DIRECTED ■ GUIDED ■ INDEPENDENT

Track Your Progress

Big Idea Fossils help us understand Earth's history.

Essential Questions

Now I Get the Big Idea!

Science Notebook

Before you begin each lesson, be sure to write your thoughts about the Essential Question.

Essential Question

What Are Fossils?

Engage Your Brain!

Find the answer to the following question in this lesson and record it here.

These animals no longer live on Earth. What can scientists learn about Earth's history by studying these animals?

_____

_____

_____

_____

Active Reading

Lesson Vocabulary

List the terms. As you learn about each one, make notes in the Interactive Glossary.

_____

_____

_____

Main Ideas

The main idea of a paragraph is the most important idea. The main idea may be stated in the first sentence, or it may be stated elsewhere. Active readers look for main ideas by asking themselves, What is this section mostly about?

Fossils— Hard or Soft

A seashell is evidence of an animal living today. But what about if you find what looks like a seashell inside a rock?

Active Reading As you read these two pages, underline how the soft parts of an organism can become a fossil.

The preserved remains or traces of a living thing is called a **fossil**. Fossils can be tracks or marks made by the organism. Fossils can also be made of an organism's hard parts, such as its bones, teeth, or shell.

All living things have carbon. Some soft parts get preserved as *carbon films* in rock.

Footprints show that an animal was there, even though none of its parts were preserved.

142

Soft parts, such as skin and organs, are rare as fossils because they quickly break down. Soft-part fossils can be original tissue if it has been frozen or dried out as in a mummy. They can also be preserved as an impression in a rock.

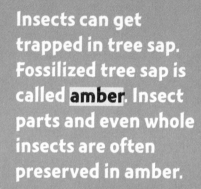

Sometimes, whole organisms can be preserved as fossils. This baby mammoth was frozen in ice. Its soft tissues were preserved along with its bones and teeth.

Insects can get trapped in tree sap. Fossilized tree sap is called **amber**. Insect parts and even whole insects are often preserved in amber.

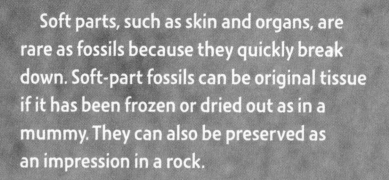

Leave a Trace

Draw footprints or other marks that you might leave that could become a fossil. What part of your body would make it? What could future scientists tell from studying it?

_____

_____

_____

Fossil Formation

Not every living thing makes a fossil. How do fossils form?

As you read the next page, circle two clue words that signal a sequence or order.

Having teeth, bones, a shell, or other hard body parts does not mean that an animal will leave a fossil. Something must happen after the organism dies. The chance of becoming a fossil is higher if the organism is buried.

One common way that fossils form is shown below.

1. An animal dies and settles on the bottom of a body of water.

2. Sediment buries the animal. Over time, the soft parts of the animal decay.

3. Hard parts are preserved in sediment as a fossil.

A mold and cast fossil forms differently. First, a leaf is pressed into soft mud. It leaves a hollow space called a mold. Then, the mold fills with mud. The mud hardens to form a cast.

Another way fossils form occurs as minerals, such as quartz, replace the shell or plant material. This is how *petrified* wood forms. Sometimes, the replacement is so perfect that you can even see the bark and wood grain!

▶ Why do animals in the water have a better chance to become fossils than animals on land?

_____

_____

_____

Fossil Features

What do scientists do when they find fossils?

Active Reading On the next page, draw boxes around things that are being compared.

When scientists find a fossil, they need a way to identify it. They can compare the fossil to other fossils. They can also compare the fossil to living organisms that are similar. Artists can use information about the living organisms to make drawings and models of what the creature might have looked like.

Giant ground sloths once lived in North America. They ate twigs and leaves that they stripped from trees using their long claws. Scientists can tell they were mammals by comparing their bones to those of modern mammals.

Sometimes, comparing a fossil to a living creature helps to show something the organisms share. But sometimes, a comparison shows how the organisms might look the same but still be very different.

Brachiopods are small sea animals without backbones. Their fossils show that they have two shells. Brachiopods look a little bit like clams.

Seed ferns were plants that lived on Earth long ago. Their fossils may look like modern ferns, but modern ferns do not bear seeds!

▶ Look at the bryozoan fossil. If it were found near brachiopod fossils, what environment would you expect bryozoans to live in?

_____

_____

What Fossils Tell Us

jawless fish

armored fish

Fossils can tell us a lot about what life on Earth was like in the past.

Active Reading Circle the name of the organism shown that has changed the least over time.

Scientists who study fossils are called **paleontologists**. Fossils show that some types of plants and animals have changed a lot. Other plants and animals have hardly changed at all.

The woolly mammoth is related to modern elephants. It lived during the last Ice Age. Today's elephants live mostly in warm climates.

modern fish

The first fish had no jaws. Some had armored plates. Over time, fish developed jaws. Today, few fish that have jaws also have armored plates.

The ginkgo tree has existed for around 200 million years. The leaves of today's ginkgos look very similar to those that grew long ago.

Do the Math!
Use a Data Table

Look at the data table to see about how many years ago the animal became extinct. Then answer the question.

Animal	Years Ago
woolly mammoth	3,700
short-faced bear	11,000
dire wolf	11,700

What is the difference between when the dire wolf became extinct and when the woolly mammoth became extinct?

_____

_____

Evidence of Environments

How do fossils serve as evidence for past environments?

Active Reading Underline two things that you can tell from studying rocks and fossils in an area.

You can learn about an area's history by studying its rocks and fossils. For example, you can tell how living things in that area changed over time. You can also tell how environments changed in that area. For example, each rock layer of the Grand Canyon formed at a different time and in a different environment. The types of fossils in each layer help show what the environment was like at that time.

© Houghton Mifflin Harcourt Publishing Company (bg) ©imac/Alamy

The fossils in this layer of rock show that they were formed in an ocean.

This layer of rock is older than the layers above it. It contains a fossil imprint, or mold, of a plant.

Fossils like these are found in another layer of rock also formed in the ocean.

▶ What does the fossil of the plant tell about the environment for that rock layer?

_____

_____

_____

This layer of rock is one of the lower layers of the canyon and is older than all of the rocks above. It contains fossils of trilobites, small animals like horseshoe crabs, that lived in ancient seas.

When you're done, use the answer key to check and revise your work.

Complete the outline below to summarize part of the lesson.

Summarize

I. Fossils—Hard or Soft

   A. Fossils are the preserved parts or traces of past life.

   B. Examples of Fossils

      1. preserved in amber or ice

      2. mold and cast fossils

      3. carbon film or footprints

II. How Fossils Form

   A. Common Process

      1. Organisms die and settle on the bottom of a lake or ocean.

      2. _____.

      3. _____.

   B. Petrification involves replacement of shell or plant material

   with _____.

III. What Fossils Tell Us

   A. Scientists called _____ study fossils.

   B. How life has changed on Earth

   C. How _____ have changed over time

Name _____

Word Play

1 Fill in the missing letters in each word. You will use each of the letters in the box.

> A F G H I L L
> M O O P R S T

1. F___S___IL
2. P___LE___N___OLO___IST
3. ___INE___A___S
4. S___EL___
5. ___OOT___R___NT

Fill in the blanks with the correct word from above.

6. A _____ is a scientist who studies fossils.

7. Although not part of an organism, a _____ is still a fossil.

8. A _____ can become a fossil because it is a hard part of the organism.

9. The preserved remains or traces of a once-living organism is a _____.

10. Petrified wood forms when _____ replace the plant material in a piece of wood.

Apply Concepts

2 Number the diagrams in the correct order to show how fossils can form.

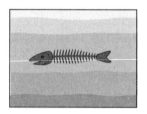 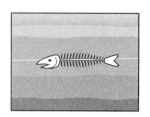 

_____   _____   _____

3 Which would have a better chance of becoming a fossil: a fish that dies and settles to the ocean floor or a mouse that dies on the ground in a forest? Explain your answer.

_____

_____

4 While hiking in the mountains, Carla finds a trilobite fossil. Is the fossil evidence of a past organism? What can she conclude about the environment from the fossil? Construct an argument to explain your ideas.

_____

_____

_____

_____

Take It Home!

See *ScienceSaurus*® for more information about Earth's history and fossils.

Name _____

Essential Question

How Do Fossils Form?

Set a Purpose

What will you learn from this experiment?

_____

_____

_____

Think About the Procedure

1. What do you expect to happen when you press the shell into the clay? State your prediction.

_____

_____

_____

_____

2. Why is petroleum jelly used?

_____

_____

_____

Record Your Data

In the space below, make a drawing of the clay and the glue after you separate them.

155

Draw Conclusions

Relate your model to the steps of how a fossil can form.

_____

_____

_____

_____

Analyze and Extend

1. Does your model help to explain fossil footprints? Explain your reasoning.

_____

_____

_____

_____

2. How does a fossil made in this way limit what you can learn about the organism?

_____

_____

_____

_____

3. While on a walk, you see some animal tracks. How could you use liquid plaster to make a record of the tracks?

_____

_____

_____

_____

4. What other questions do you have about how fossils form?

_____

_____

_____

_____

Meet Some Paleontology Pioneers

Luis and Walter Alvarez

In 1980, a father-and-son team had an idea. The Alvarezes examined a rock layer that formed when dinosaurs became extinct around 65 million years ago. Material in the rock matched what is usually found in asteroids. It seemed that an asteroid had hit Earth! The Alvarezes hypothesized that the crash sent dust into the air that blocked sunlight. Now many scientists agree!

Karen Chin

Karen Chin knows that we learn about animals by studying what they eat. That is why she studies the fossils of dinosaur dung! She can tell how they interacted with other animals and plants. Dr. Chin was the first person to identify and study *Tyrannosaurus rex* poop! She showed that *Tyrannosaurus rex* ate other dinosaurs—bones and all.

Describe Dinosaurs

Look at each skeleton below. Answer the questions to compare and contrast the dinosaurs.

Stegosaurus

What do you think the plates on *Stegosaurus*'s back were for?

_____

_____

Why do you think *Stegosaurus*'s tail was so long?

_____

_____

_____

What do you think *Tyrannosaurus rex* ate? Why do you think so?

_____

_____

Tyrannosaurus rex

Why do you think *Tyrannosaurus rex*'s legs were longer than its arms?

_____

_____

_____

How do scientists find data to answer these questions?

_____

_____

_____

What do scientists learn from locations of dinosaur fossils?

_____

_____

How It Works:
Walk This Way

Scientists measure the distance between fossil footprints. They study dinosaur joints in fossil skeletons. Scientists use these data with the aid of computers to see what a walking dinosaur would have looked like.

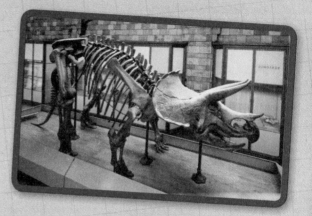

A computer model starts with a skeleton. Then virtual muscles are added. Finally scientists are able to animate *Triceratops* in motion.

Troubleshooting

Study the pictures of the walking *Triceratops* below. Describe how it moves.

_____

_____

S.T.E.M.
continued

Before movie cameras and computers, people studied animal motion by taking a rapid series of still photographs. They could look at the pictures in order to understand the animal's motion.

This famous set of images shows how a horse gallops. At one point in its stride, a horse has all four feet in the air. Write another detail that you observe about how the horse moves.

_____

_____

Research how a hummingbird flies. Draw separate images of a hummingbird in flight. How is high-speed video of hummingbirds shot?

_____

_____

_____

Build On It!

Rise to the engineering design challenge—complete **Make a Process: Design a Fossil Exhibit Hall** in the Inquiry Flipchart.

© Houghton Mifflin Harcourt Publishing Company (t) ©Mary Evans Picture Library/Alamy; (b) ©Francois Gohier/Photo Researchers, Inc.

Unit 4 Review

Vocabulary Review

Use the terms in the box to complete the sentences.

> amber
> fossil
> paleontologist

1. The remains or traces of a plant or animal that lived long ago is a(n) _____.

2. A scientist who studies the remains of an ancient organism is called a(n) _____.

3. Insects can be seen in fossilized tree sap called _____.

Science Concepts

Fill in the letter of the choice that best answers the question.

4. Not every animal or plant becomes a fossil when it dies. Which event **best** helps a fossil form?

   Ⓐ Water washes away dirt.

   Ⓑ Animals eat the soft tissues.

   Ⓒ Wind blows the dead organism away.

   Ⓓ Sediment quickly buries the dead organism.

5. A jellyfish has no hard body parts. Which statement **best** describes how a fossil of a jellyfish could form?

   Ⓐ The body of the jellyfish is frozen.

   Ⓑ The jellyfish changes into a carbon film.

   Ⓒ The jellyfish becomes trapped in amber.

   Ⓓ The bones of the jellyfish are replaced by minerals.

Science Concepts

Fill in the letter of the choice that best answers the question.

6. Nkomo found a piece of amber. Which object shown below would the amber most likely contain?

Ⓐ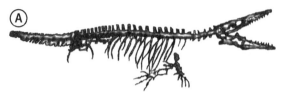

Ⓑ

Ⓒ

Ⓓ

7. Malaya was collecting fossils. She found one whose original material had been replaced by quartz. What did she find?

Ⓐ trace fossil
Ⓑ carbon film
Ⓒ petrified wood
Ⓓ mummified body

8. Suppose you found fossils of sharks and other fish in a nearby forest. What could you infer about the area from these discoveries?

Ⓐ The area was once a desert.
Ⓑ The area was once an ocean.
Ⓒ The area was once a forest.
Ⓓ The area was once an ice field.

9. Antarctica is located at the South Pole. It is cold and mostly covered by snow and ice. Scientists have found fossils of warm-water marine reptiles on a mountain in Antarctica. What is the best argument to make based on the evidence?

Ⓐ The rock layer with the fossils was formed when the area was a warm, shallow sea.
Ⓑ The reptiles were washed up onto the land, where they were covered and became fossils.
Ⓒ The reptiles were frozen in ice and were found after the ice melted.
Ⓓ A storm caused the reptiles to become lost, and they died in the cold waters.

10. Look at the diagram of the rock layers with fossils.

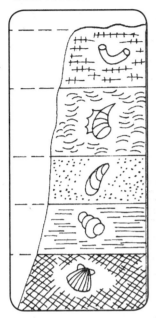

What conclusion is **best** supported by the diagram?

Ⓐ The environment was a tropical forest when the bottom layer of rock was formed.

Ⓑ The organisms showed the least amount of change between the third and fourth layers from the top.

Ⓒ There was little change in the types of organisms present between the bottom and top layers.

Ⓓ The environment in the area was the same when the rock layers formed as it is today.

11. Which fossil does not include a part of an organism?

Ⓐ a shark's tooth

Ⓑ a worm's burrow

Ⓒ a mammal's bone

Ⓓ a dinosaur's egg

12. Organisms that look as if they have not changed much over time are sometimes called living fossils. Which organism best fits this description?

Ⓐ ginkgo trees

Ⓑ elephants

Ⓒ tree ferns

Ⓓ fish

13. Which describes the most likely way soft parts of an organism can form a fossil?

Ⓐ The organism is eaten by another organism and is preserved in its stomach.

Ⓑ The organism is buried long after it has died and minerals replace the soft parts.

Ⓒ The organism dies by falling into a deep, dry hole and becomes a mummy.

Ⓓ The organism is covered by lava, which then cools and hardens.

Apply Inquiry and Review the Big Idea

Write the answers to these questions.

14. Two third graders are planning to give a presentation about fossils to the class.

a. Ronda must explain how scientists use fossils as evidence of past environments. Write at least two things that she should include in her presentation.

_____

_____

_____

_____

_____

_____

b. Gabe must explain how scientists use fossils found in areas such as the Grand Canyon to demonstrate how life forms have changed over time. Write three things that Gabe should include in his presentation.

_____

_____

_____

_____

_____

_____

UNIT 5
Heat Energy

Big Idea

Heat energy can be transferred.

S3P1., S3P1.a, S3P1.b, S3P1.c

Lightning strikes over Miami, Florida

I Wonder Why

Lightning is bright. But lightning also sometimes starts fires. Why? *Turn the page to find out.*

Here's Why Lightning gives off light, but it also gives off heat. The temperature of a lightning bolt can be hotter than the surface of the sun! No wonder it can set things on fire.

Levels of Inquiry Key ■ DIRECTED ■ GUIDED ■ INDEPENDENT

Big Idea Heat energy can be transferred.

Track Your Progress

Essential Questions

Science Notebook

Before you begin each lesson, be sure to write your thoughts about the Essential Question.

Essential Question

What Are Some Heat Sources?

Engage Your Brain!

Find the answer to the following question in this lesson and record it here.

The brakes on a car rub against the wheels to stop the car. But why are this car's brakes bright orange?

_____

_____

_____

Active Reading

Lesson Vocabulary

List the terms. As you learn about each one, make notes in the Interactive Glossary.

_____

_____

Main Idea

The main idea of a section is the most important idea. The main idea may be stated in the first sentence, or it may be stated elsewhere. Active readers look for main ideas by asking themselves, What is this section mostly about?

Sharing the Warmth

Here are two common words: heat and temperature. You hear them every day. But what do they really mean?

Active Reading As you read these two pages, circle the clue word or phrase that signals a detail such as an example or an added fact.

Scientists use words very carefully. Some common words have special meanings in science. For example, when you use the word *heat*, you might mean how warm something is. In science, **heat** is energy that moves from warmer objects to cooler objects.

The temperature of the water in these hot springs is higher than the temperature of the monkeys. Heat flows from the warmer water to the monkeys. The monkeys feel warmer.

Temperature is the measure of how hot or cold something is. Temperature can be measured in degrees. Water with a temperature of 32 °C (90 °F) is hotter than water with a temperature of 12 °C (54 °F).

Remember, heat is energy. Heat always moves from an object with a higher temperature to one with a lower temperature.

Heat Can Move

In each picture, heat will flow from one object to another. Draw an arrow to show which way it will flow.

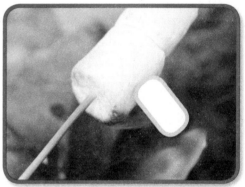

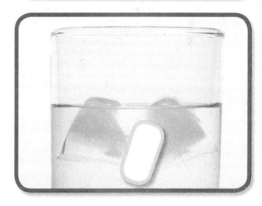

The red part of the metal horseshoe has a very high temperature. Heat moved from the fire into the red part of the horseshoe.

Turn Up the Heat

Heat moves from something warmer to something cooler. You rely on that every day. How? Here is just one way.

Active Reading As you read these two pages, underline signal words that identify sequence.

Would you like to eat nothing but raw food? Ugh! For things to cook, they must gain heat energy.

Heat moves from the blue flames to the pot. Then it moves from the pot to the stew. The heat cooks the stew.

1 This oven is used to bake food. Heat moves from the oven to the air inside the oven. Then it moves from the hot air to the food. The heat from the oven baked these cookies!

2 Some things slow the movement of heat. The woman in the picture is using oven mitts. The mitts slow the movement of heat, so she does not get burned.

Do the Math!
Read a Table

1. What foods are cooked at 145 °F?

_____

2. Which food needs to be cooked at a higher temperature, eggs or chicken?

_____

3. What food is cooked at 160 °F?

_____

Safe Food Cooking Temperatures

Type of Food	Cooking Temperature
Eggs	160 °F
Salmon	145 °F
Beef	145 °F
Chicken	165 °F

Hot Light

Have you ever touched a light bulb that had been on for a while? The heat may have surprised you!

Active Reading As you read these two pages, draw a star next to what you consider to be the most important sentence, and be ready to explain why.

Old-fashioned light bulbs give off heat. Some newer kinds give off more light and less heat.

You've learned that heat is energy. But remember, light is a form of energy, too. Heat and light often occur together. Many things that give off light also often give off heat.

The light bulb is used for its light, but it also gives off heat. The coil inside a toaster gives off heat. That's how the bread gets toasted. But the coil also gives off an orange-red light. When something gives off both light and heat, we often want to use just one or the other.

It's not unusual to see something glowing red and giving off heat. That's what the lava is doing in this picture.

The sun gives off light, and it also gives off heat. We need both to survive.

Heat and Light Sources

How many things in your house give off light and heat? List some of them here.

_____

_____

_____

_____

The charcoal is giving off orange light. It also gives off the heat that cooks the meat.

The light from a candle's flame can let us see in a dark room. The heat from the flame melts the wax.

Burn Rubber

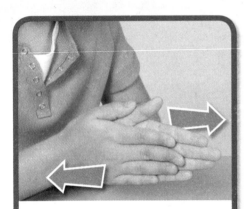

If you're ever out in the cold without gloves, rub your hands together. The heat you produce will warm your hands!

Q: Can you make a fire by rubbing two sticks together?
A: Yes, if one of them is a match!

That's an old joke, so you may have heard it before. However, you actually can make a fire by rubbing two sticks together. You have to move them quickly, and you must have something nearby to burn. But it can be done. Where do you think the heat comes from?

Active Reading As you read these two pages, draw circles around two words or phrases that are key to understanding the main idea.

The tires are rubbing against the road as they spin. They're spinning very quickly and producing a lot of heat. They're getting so hot that they're burning. That's where the smoke is coming from.

When two things rub against each other, there is *friction* [FRIK•shuhn] where they touch. Friction produces heat. The faster and harder the two things rub, the more heat is produced.

Where Is Heat Produced?

In each photo, two things are rubbing together to produce heat. Draw a circle around the point where the heat is being produced. Then write a caption for each picture.

Sum It Up!

When you're done, use the answer key to check and revise your work.

Write the correct word in the blank.

1

Things that give off

_____

often give off heat as well.

2

_____

is measured in degrees.

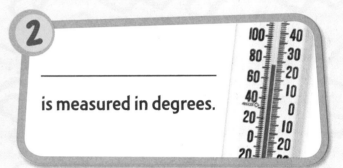

Complete the graphic organizer.

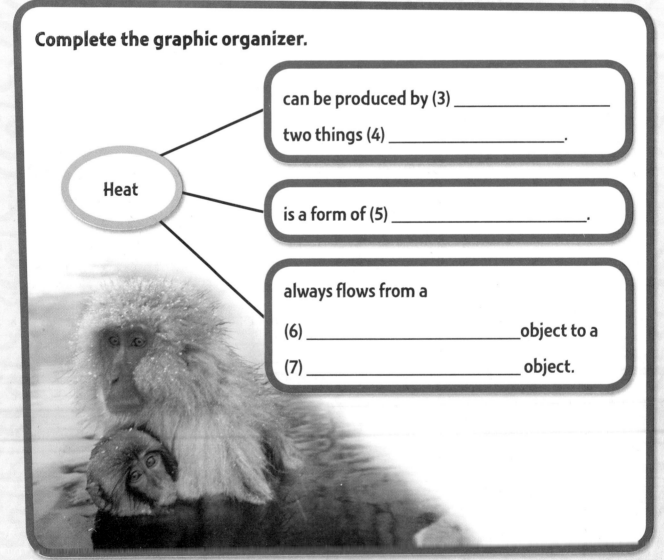

Heat

can be produced by (3) _____

two things (4) _____.

is a form of (5) _____.

always flows from a

(6) _____ object to a

(7) _____ object.

Answer Key: 1. light 2. Temperature 3. rubbing 4. together 5. energy 6. warmer 7. cooler

Name _____

Word Play

1 Use the clues to help unscramble each word. Write the unscrambled word in the boxes.

Something with a higher temperature is
ETHOTR

Something that is hot may do this.
WLGO

The measure of how hot or cold something is
MTEEERPUTAR

Friction from spinning race car tires might cause this.
MKSOE

This produces heat when two things rub together.
ITRNFICO

Something with a very low temperature is this.
OCDL

Unscramble the letters in the circles to form a word that is related to this lesson.

Apply Concepts

2 Circle the object that can give off heat but not light.

sun

candle

hot chocolate

3 Name two things you sometimes do to prevent heat from being transferred.

_____

_____

_____

4 Name two things that give off both light and heat.

_____

5 Name one way that you use heat.

_____

Take It Home! With your family, pick two rooms in your home. Go through the rooms, looking for everything that produces light. For each thing you find, discuss if that thing also produces heat.

Name _____

Essential Question

Where Can Heat Come From?

Set a Purpose

What do you think is the purpose of this investigation?

_____

_____

_____

_____

Think About the Procedure

Why are you using different items to rub together?

_____

_____

_____

_____

Record Your Data

Record your results in the table below.

Setup	Hot?	Observations
hands rubbed against each other		
cloths rubbed against each other		
paper rubbed against **wood** with **nothing** between them		
paper rubbed against **wood** with **dish soap** between them		

179

Draw Conclusions

Compare your results with the other groups. What do you find?

_____

_____

Why might this be the case?

_____

_____

Analyze and Extend

1. If two parts of a machine rub together, what could you do to keep them from getting as hot?

_____

_____

_____

_____

2. How would you plan an investigation to find possible materials to reduce friction?

_____

_____

_____

_____

_____

3. Look at the setup below. Ramp 1 has a smooth surface. Ramp 2 has a sandpaper surface. Will the book on either ramp move? Explain.

Ramp 1

Ramp 2

_____

_____

_____

_____

_____

4. What other questions would you like to ask about how heat can be produced?

_____

_____

_____

_____

Ask a Volcanologist

Q. What does a volcanologist do?

A. A volcanologist is a person who studies volcanoes. We can warn people when a volcano will erupt. People will have time to get to safety.

Q. How do you stay safe when working around lava?

A. I wear special clothes, gloves, and boots to protect me from the heat. I wear a gas mask to protect me from volcanic gases.

Q. How do you know that lava is very hot?

A. Lava is very hot! You know that lava is hot because it gives off heat and light. It may glow bright orange, yellow, or red.

Now It's Your Turn!

What question would you ask a volcanologist?

_____

_____

_____

_____

Careers in Science continued

Be a Volcanologist

Volcanologists can tell lava's temperature by the color it glows.

Match each temperature below to the lava flowing from the volcano. Write the temperature in the correct location.

1100°C	bright orange
850°C	bright red
650°C	dark red
200°C	black

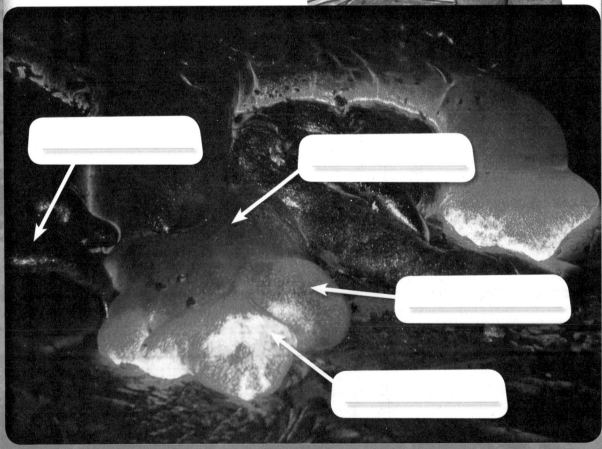

Essential Question

How Does Sunlight Affect Objects?

Engage Your Brain!

Find the answer to the following question in this lesson and record it here.

What are three things that can happen to sunlight when it strikes an object?

_____

_____

_____

Active Reading

Lesson Vocabulary
List the terms. As you learn about each one, make notes in the Interactive Glossary.

_____

_____

Compare and Contrast
Many ideas in this lesson are connected because they explain comparisons and contrasts—how things are alike and different. Active readers stay focused on comparisons and contrasts when they ask themselves, How are these things alike? How are they different?

Heating Up

Have you ever heard, "It's hot enough to fry an egg on the sidewalk?" What effect does sunlight have on things?

Active Reading As you read these two pages, circle signal words that identify cause and effect.

The sun gives off light and heat. On a cool day, you might enjoy standing in the sun. When sunlight shines on you, it gives some of its energy to you. As a result, you warm up. But on a hot day, you might prefer to sit in the shade with a cool drink.

It is not an egg, but this fruit bar does not do well on a sunny sidewalk! Sunlight warms the fruit bar and the sidewalk. As a result, the fruit bar melts into a big, messy puddle.

Do the Math!

Make a Graph

The table shows the temperature of putty that was left in the sun. Graph these data.

Time	Temperature (°C)
12:00	26
12:05	28
12:10	31
12:15	33
12:20	35

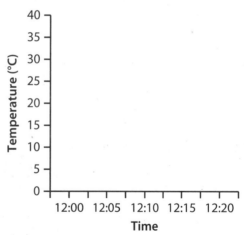

Explain what the graph shows about the effect of sunlight.

_____

_____

_____

Sunlight Hits It, and Then ...

The cat casts a shadow, but the glass in the window doesn't. What's going on?

Whether an object casts a shadow depends on how sunlight interacts with it.

Sunlight Passes Through

The window lets sunlight pass through. The light shines into the house. It will warm objects that it shines on, including the cat! Light also passes through the air on each side of the window.

Active Reading As you read these two pages, underline three ways that sunlight interacts with objects.

When you "soak up some rays," you absorb sunlight.

Sunlight Is Absorbed

The cat makes a shadow. The sunlight does not pass through the cat! Some of the sunlight hitting the cat is **absorbed**, or taken in, by the cat. This transfers energy to the cat and warms it. The more energy that is absorbed by an object, the faster it can warm up.

Sunlight Is Reflected

Some of the sunlight hitting the cat **reflects** or bounces off of the cat. This reflected light is what lets you see the cat. But to reflect most of the light requires something smooth and shiny, such as a mirror.

These mirrors reflect sunlight to heat sodium metal until it melts.

▶ Identify how light interacts with each material.

plastic wrap

aluminum foil

_____   _____

Cool Colors, Hot Hues

Does color make a difference in how sunlight affects objects?

Look at the road and the sidewalk. Which would you rather walk on when it is hot and sunny? The black surface of the road can become much hotter than the sidewalk. Darker colors absorb more sunlight that shines on them. Lighter colors reflect more sunlight than darker colors. So, they absorb less sunlight than darker colors.

In the summer, lighter-colored clothes help keep you cooler. In the winter, darker colors can help you stay warmer.

Active Reading As you read these two pages, underline two sentences that state the main idea.

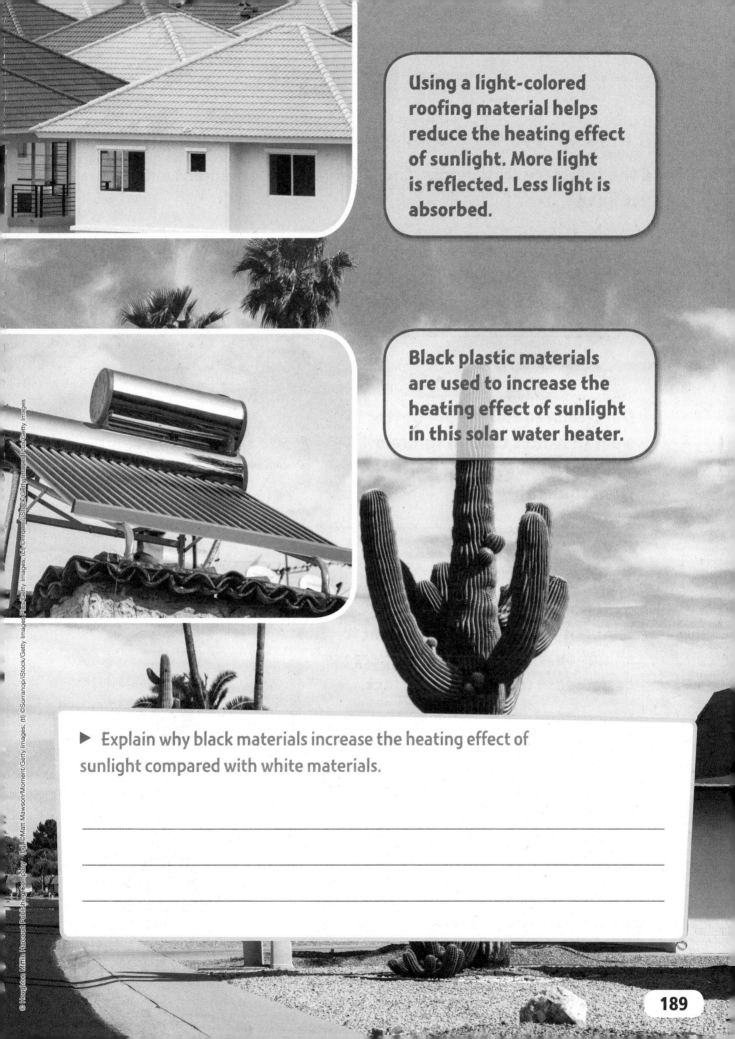

Using a light-colored roofing material helps reduce the heating effect of sunlight. More light is reflected. Less light is absorbed.

Black plastic materials are used to increase the heating effect of sunlight in this solar water heater.

▶ Explain why black materials increase the heating effect of sunlight compared with white materials.

_____

_____

_____

When you're done, use the answer key to check and revise your work.

Read the summary statements. Then match each statement with the correct image.

A

1 Some materials reflect sunlight, so the light bounces off.

_____

2 Dark-colored clothes are better to wear in winter than in summer. Dark colors absorb more energy from sunlight.

_____

B

3 Sunlight heats up an object that it shines on. There are ways to increase or decrease this warming effect.

_____

C

4 Some materials allow sunlight to pass through and warm things on the other side.

_____

D

Answer Key: 1.B 2.D 3.A 4.C

Name _____

Word Play

1 **Use the clues to help you unscramble the words below.**

1. lectrefs   _____   What an object does to light when light bounces off

2. mortertheme   _____   The tool that lets you measure the heating effect of the sun

3. robsbas   _____   What an object does to light when light gets soaked up

4. thiew   _____   A color that can help reduce the heating effect of the sun

5. ptuemrareet   _____   This increases when something is sitting in a sunny spot

6. thusling   _____   Has a heating effect when it shines on things

2 The data table shows the temperature of a picnic table in a park in the evening. Make a graph of these data.

Time	Temperature (°F)
8:00	95
8:30	91
9:00	86
9:30	80
10:00	73

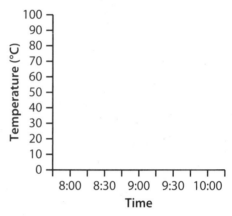

Explain what the graph shows about the effect of sunlight.

_____

_____

3 Four houses are on the same street. Circle the house that will get hot fastest in the morning.

4 Explain why you chose the house you circled. Why do you expect it to get hot fastest?

_____

_____

Take It Home!

Plan and carry out an investigation on the effect of sunlight in your home. Use a thermometer, several different objects, and a sunny spot. Record the temperature over time and graph it. Share what you find with a friend or family member.

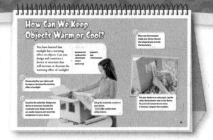

Name _____

Essential Question

How Can We Keep Objects Warm or Cool?

Set a Purpose
What will you learn from this experiment?

_____

_____

_____

Think About the Procedure
1. **What do you expect to happen if more sunlight is absorbed by an object? State your prediction.**

_____

_____

_____

2. **Do you plan to design something to increase or decrease the warming effect of sunlight?**

_____

_____

_____

Record Your Data
In the space below, make a drawing of your device. Label the materials that you used.

Draw Conclusions

Describe how your device or structure increases (or decreases) the warming effect of the sun.

_____

_____

_____

_____

Analyze and Extend

1. How well did your device or structure work? Explain your reasoning.

_____

_____

_____

_____

2. Compare your device or structure with those of other students. Describe an additional change that you could make to your design that would improve it.

_____

_____

_____

3. Imagine that you work for a company that designs products for the outdoors. Describe how your device could be used.

_____

_____

_____

_____

4. Imagine that your first product is a hit, and the company wants your ideas for a new device that has the opposite effect. What are some different materials you would suggest for the new device?

_____

_____

_____

_____

5. What other questions do you have about how to increase or decrease the warming effect of the sun?

_____

_____

_____

_____

Warm It Up

Compare Greenhouses

Greenhouses are made of glass or plastic. Glass and plastic let in light. They also keep in heat. Light and heat help plants grow. Different plants can be grown at the same time.

| indoor greenhouse | outdoor greenhouse |

- needs only a small space
- for small plants only
- stays warm in winter

- needs a large space
- for small or large plants
- needs heating in winter

Which Greenhouse?

Read the sentences below.
Then answer the questions.

You want to grow a large plant. You have a lot of outdoor space, and you live in an area where the weather is not very cold. Which greenhouse would you choose? Why is this the best choice?

_____

_____

_____

_____

_____

Build On It!

Design your own indoor greenhouse. Complete **Design It: Greenhouse** on the Inquiry Flipchart.

Name _____

Vocabulary Review

Use the terms in the box to complete the sentences.

1. The _____ of an object is a measure of how hot or cold the object is.

2. Energy that moves from warmer objects to cooler objects is _____.

Science Concepts

Fill in the letter of the choice that best answers the question.

3. Lucas is having a birthday party. He has ice cream, balloons, and a cake with candles.

Which of the objects shown in the picture produces the most heat?

Ⓐ cake

Ⓑ candles

Ⓒ balloon

Ⓓ ice cream

4. Hiroto wants to warm a pot of soup on a stove. He will put the pot onto one of the stove's heat elements and turn it on .

Heat elements

Which heat element does Hiroto know is very hot, without touching them?

Ⓐ the biggest one

Ⓑ the smallest one

Ⓒ the one that glows red

Ⓓ the one that looks dark

Science Concepts

Fill in the letter of the choice that best answers the question.

5. Sandra's mother is boiling water on a stove. In which picture does the arrow show the direction that heat moves to make the water boil?

Ⓐ

Ⓑ

Ⓒ

Ⓓ

6. Nolan picks up a book from his desk and hands it to his teacher. His teacher sets the book down and slides it across a table. Which action produces the most heat?

Ⓐ sliding the book across a table

Ⓑ handing the book to his teacher

Ⓒ setting the book down on a table

Ⓓ picking the book up from his desk

7. Marvin and Byron both hold a thermometer close to a light bulb. After 2 minutes, they record their measurement. Marvin records 67 °C. Byron records 65 °C. Why might they have different results?

Ⓐ The light bulb is not the same temperature on all sides.

Ⓑ Marvin held his thermometer closer to the bulb than Byron did.

Ⓒ One of the thermometers was not working correctly.

Ⓓ Marvin read the Fahrenheit temperature instead of the Celsius temperature.

8. Jamal is toasting marshmallows over a campfire.

Which of the following signs shows that the fire is probably hot?

Ⓐ It has sticks in it.

Ⓑ It has bright flames.

Ⓒ It has ashes around it.

Ⓓ It has sand under the logs.

9. A mover pushes a box up a ramp into a truck.

Which two things become warmer when the man pushes the box?

Ⓐ box and air

Ⓑ ramp and box

Ⓒ man and truck

Ⓓ truck and ramp

10. Jason is sanding a board with sandpaper. He puts a piece of sandpaper around a block of wood and sands the board. Which of the following terms has a specific meaning in science that could relate to Jason's activity?

Ⓐ experiment

Ⓑ evidence

Ⓒ heat

Ⓓ sanding

11. Which color of shirt would help you stay cooler on a hot, sunny day?

Ⓐ purple

Ⓑ white

Ⓒ maroon

Ⓓ black

12. Matthew's class investigates friction between smooth items and rough items. They find that rough items produce more friction. Which of the following items would create the most heat if rubbed together for 20 seconds?

Ⓐ

Plastic containers

Ⓑ

Rough cardboard

Ⓒ
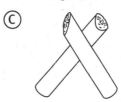
Chalk

Ⓓ
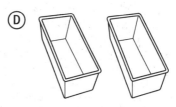
Baking pans

Apply Inquiry and Review the Big Idea

Write the answers to these questions.

13. Jenna and Tanner want to decrease the friction between a wooden block and a ramp. They have tried two objects already and will try others.

Ramp covering	How object moved	
	Faster	Slower
Plastic tablecloth	X	
Cloth tablecloth		X

a. Next, they would like to test either a plastic cover or a bed sheet. Based on the evidence they have gathered, which is **most likely** to create the least amount of friction on the ramp? Explain your answer.

_____

_____

_____

b. A block is pushed up a ramp that is covered in carpet. The same block is pushed up the same ramp that is covered with a curtain. How will the temperatures of the block after each trial compare? Explain your answer.

_____

_____

_____

14. Franco uses a thermometer to determine the effect of sunlight on different parts of a car. He measures the temperatures of the black and white sections of a tire in direct sunlight. Predict how the temperatures would compare.

_____

_____

_____

Plants and Animals

© Houghton Mifflin Harcourt Publishing Company (border) ©NDisc/Age Fotostock; (inset) ©Jeff Hunter/Getty Images; (bg) ©Pascal Kobeh/Photolibrary New York

Big Idea

Living things have adaptations that help them survive in their environments. All living, once-living, and nonliving things interact in an ecosystem.

S3L1, S3L1.a, S3L1.b, S3L1.c, S3L2.a, S3L2.b

mantis shrimp

I Wonder Why

Why is this mantis shrimp these colors? *Turn the page to find out.*

Here's Why The colorful shell of the mantis shrimp helps it blend in with its surroundings. Blending in helps the mantis shrimp hide from predators and surprise prey.

In this unit, you will explore the Big Idea, the Essential Questions, and the Investigations on the Inquiry Flipchart.

Levels of Inquiry Key ■ DIRECTED ■ GUIDED ■ INDEPENDENT

Track Your Progress

Big Idea Living things have adaptations that help them survive in their environments. All living, once-living, and nonliving things interact in an ecosystem.

Essential Questions

Now I Get the Big Idea!

Science Notebook
Before you begin each lesson, be sure to write your thoughts about the Essential Question.

Essential Question

What Are Some Adaptations of Animals?

Engage Your Brain!

Find the answer to the following question in this lesson and record it here.

Why is the pelican's beak so large?

_____

_____

_____

_____

Active Reading

Lesson Vocabulary

List the terms. As you learn about each one, make notes in the Interactive Glossary.

_____

_____

_____

Visual Aids

Pictures and their captions add information to the text on a page. Active readers pause their reading to review pictures and captions, then decide how the information in the pictures and captions adds to what is provided in the text.

203

Staying Alive

Life in the wild isn't easy. Animals must survive in the environment where they live. Their adaptations help them stay alive.

Active Reading As you read these two pages, draw a line from the adaptation shown in each picture to the words that describe it.

An **adaptation** is any trait that helps a living thing survive. Animals that are hunted for food are called *prey*. Animals that hunt prey are called *predators*. Predators and prey have adaptations that help them catch food or avoid being eaten. Animals have other kinds of adaptations, too.

What animal is this? It has flat teeth. The flat teeth allow it to grind grass.

The tiger eats animals such as wild boar and deer. The tiger's sharp teeth help it tear meat.

The arctic hare lives in snow and ice. Less heat escapes from its small ears than from the larger ears of other hares. Its small ears help it stay warm in the cold.

The jackrabbit lives in the desert. Its long ears contain many tiny blood vessels that help remove heat from its body. This helps the jackrabbit keep cool in the heat.

Guess Who?

A finch has a beak that it uses to crack seeds and nuts. An eagle uses its beak to tear meat for food. Which bird's beak is shown in photo 1? In photo 2?

1. _____

2. _____

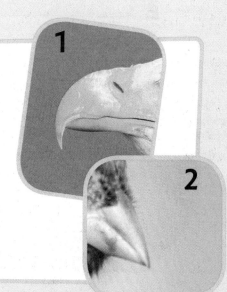

Staying Safe

Look out! It's a predator! Some adaptations help animals defend themselves without fighting.

Active Reading As you read these two pages, find and underline examples of defense adaptations.

Defense adaptations may attack a predator's sense of sight, smell, taste, touch, or hearing. A bad taste, loud noise, or nasty odor is often enough to make the predator go away.

A porcupine raises its quills. It swings its tail. One good strike pokes the quills into the attacker's skin. Ouch!

A skunk's spray has a bad odor. Even skunks dislike the smell! The spray also burns the eyes. It's a powerful defense against predators.

This caterpillar eats milkweed. The milkweed makes the caterpillar taste bad to birds. The pattern of stripes on the caterpillar is a warning to birds. It tells the birds that they don't want to eat it.

The frilled lizard hisses with open jaws. Its frill opens wide. It's a scary sight that frightens some predators away.

Sound the Alarm!

Like pet dogs, prairie dogs bark when they sense danger. How does this adaptation help them survive?

_____

_____

Creature Costumes

Now you see it. Now you don't. Now you see it—but it looks like something else!

Active Reading As you read these two pages, find and underline the names of two adaptations that involve an animal's appearance.

Some animals can hide without trying. These animals are hidden by their shapes, colors, or patterns. Such disguises are called **camouflage** [KAM•uh•flazh].

Some harmless animals look a lot like animals that are harmful to predators or that taste bad. Since predators don't know which animal is harmful, neither animal gets eaten. Imitating the look of another animal is called **mimicry**.

Look at the color of this snow leopard's fur. Look at its spots. Its camouflage helps it blend into the background of snow and rock. This helps it sneak up on prey.

This orchid mantis is the same color as the flower it's sitting on. The insect is perfectly camouflaged!

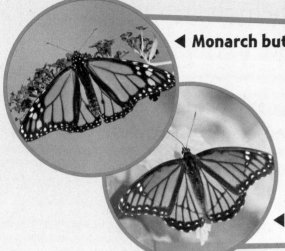

◀ **Monarch butterfly**

Eating monarch butterflies makes birds sick. Birds avoid eating them. The viceroy looks like the monarch, so birds leave them alone, too.

◀ **Viceroy butterfly**

The frogfish can look like a rock or a sponge. It can look like algae. Animals try to rest on the "rock." Others try to eat the "algae." The frogfish traps and eats them!

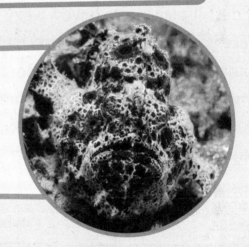

Make It Blend!

Color the lizard so that it is hidden on the leaf. On the line below, identify whether this is camouflage or mimicry.

_____

Plant Facts

Plants have adaptations that help them survive, too. How? Read more to find out!

Active Reading As you read these two pages, draw a line from the pictures to the words that tell how an adaptation helps a plant.

Plants need water. There isn't much water in a desert, so desert plants are adapted to hold moisture. Desert plants such as cactuses have thick stems that store water. The leaves of desert plants also have a waxy coating that helps prevent water loss. Most desert plants have spines, not leaves. Narrow spines help prevent water vapor from escaping from the plant. The spines also keep animals from eating the plants. Other plants have different adaptations that help them survive.

Pitcher plants can't get the nutrients they need from soil. The plants' pitchers hold water and trap insects for food. The sides are slippery, so when insects fall into the pitchers, they can't get out! The insects are digested, providing nutrients to the plant.

Blackberries taste bitter until they are ripe. Their bitter taste is an adaptation. It stops animals from eating the berries before the seeds are old enough to produce new plants.

The stone plant blends into the background of rocks and stones. Grazing animals don't see it. Camouflage keeps it from being eaten.

Do the Math!
Solve a Word Problem

A red pitcher plant catches 3 insects each week. A green pitcher plant catches 2 insects each week. How many more insects does the red plant catch in four weeks than the green plant? Show your work.

_____

_____

_____

_____

Sum It Up!

When you're done, use the answer key to check and revise your work.

Complete the summary. Use it to complete the graphic organizer.

Summarize

(1) _____ are characteristics that help living things survive.

(2) _____ is a kind of adaptation. It helps the frogfish blend into algae and catch prey. An adaptation called

(3) _____ makes the harmless viceroy butterfly look like the harmful monarch butterfly.

Main Idea: Living things have adaptations that help them survive in their environments.

(4) Detail:	(5) Detail:	Detail: A horse has flat teeth to help it grind grass.

Answer Key: 1. Adaptations **2.** Camouflage **3.** mimicry **4.** Sample answer: Camouflage helps the frogfish stay hidden from prey. **5.** Sample answer: Mimicry protects the viceroy butterfly from predators.

212

Brain Check

Name _____

Word Play

1

Unscramble the letters to complete each clue.	
1. _____ help living things survive in their environments.	p i d t a t a n a o s
2. Some plants have adaptations that help _____ them against animals that eat them.	f e d d e n
3. _____ helps an animal blend into its surroundings.	f a m a l o g c u e
4. An adaptation that makes one organism look like another is called _____.	y i m r m c i
5. A porcupine's _____ protect it from other animals.	s i l u q l
6. Animals do not eat the _____ butterfly because it looks like the monarch butterfly.	c o i r e y v

Apply Concepts

2 Look at each picture. Write the kind of adaptation that it shows.

_____   _____

3 Draw two pictures. Show an adaptation of a plant. Show an adaptation of an animal. Construct an explanation of how each adaptation helps the plant or animal survive.

Plant Adaptation	Animal Adaptation

_____   _____

_____   _____

_____   _____

Take It Home!

Observe a plant or animal in its natural habitat. What is one of its adaptations? How does the adaptation help it survive?

Meet the Insect Scientists

Miriam Rothschild

Rothschild studied the life cycle of the flea and how it reproduces.

As a child, Miriam Rothschild collected beetles and caterpillars. Later, she studied fleas and other parasites. Parasites are living things that live on or in other living things. Rothschild studied fleas on rabbits' fur. She discovered how fleas jump. In 1952, she wrote her first book. It was called *Fleas, Flukes and Cuckoos*. In 1973, she finished a book about 30,000 different fleas.

Charles Henry Turner

Charles Turner was an entomologist, a scientist who studies insects. He studied many kinds of insects, including ants and honeybees. In 1910, he proved that honeybees can see color. The next year he proved they could also see patterns. Turner found that some ants move in circles toward their home. To honor his work with ants, scientists call this behavior "Turner's circling."

Turner showed that honeybees can see a flower's color.

The Insect Scientists

Read the timeline below. Use what you read about Rothschild and Turner to fill in each blank box.

_____

_____

_____

_____

1952 Rothschild writes her first book.

1910 Turner proves that honeybees can see color.

1908 Miriam Rothschild is born.

1907 Charles Turner writes about his study of ants.

_____

_____

_____

_____

After what year on the timeline should you add the following?

A scientist names the circles that ants make when returning home "Turner's circling."

_____

Inquiry Flipchart p. 27

Name _____

Essential Question

How Can We Model a Physical Adaptation?

Set a Purpose
What will you learn from this experiment?

_____

_____

_____

Think About the Procedure
How do you think the stickiness of the tongue will affect the number of insects the frog catches? State your prediction.

_____

_____

_____

Why do you think the pieces of paper are all the same size?

_____

_____

_____

_____

Record Your Data
Record the number of insects caught with a sticky tongue and with a wet tongue for each of your five trials.

Trial	1	2	3	4	5
Sticky tongue					
Wet tongue					

Draw Conclusions

Which is better at catching insects: a sticky tongue or a wet tongue? Why?

_____

_____

_____

_____

Analyze and Extend

1. How is a sticky tongue an example of an adaptation?

_____

_____

_____

_____

2. How would this experiment change if the insects were inside a test tube instead of on the flat desktop?

_____

_____

_____

3. Suppose you were an insect that lived in an area with many sticky-tongued frogs. What adaptation might help you survive?

_____

_____

_____

_____

4. What kind of tongue is better for catching insects? What other animals do you think might have this kind of tongue?

_____

_____

_____

_____

5. What other questions do you have about adaptations for eating?

_____

_____

_____

_____

Essential Question

What Are Behavioral Adaptations?

Engage Your Brain!

Find the answer to the following question in this lesson and record it here.

Migrating geese often fly in a V formation. How do they know when it is time to migrate?

_____

_____

_____

Active Reading

Lesson Vocabulary

List the terms. As you learn about each one, make notes in the Interactive Glossary.

_____ _____

_____ _____

_____

Compare and Contrast

Many ideas in this lesson are connected because they show comparisons and contrasts—how things are alike and how things are different. Active readers stay focused on comparisons and contrasts by asking themselves, How are these things alike? How are these things different?

Know It or Learn It?

Eating, sleeping, finding shelter, and moving from place to place. How do animals know what to do?

Active Reading As you read these two pages, circle words that tell how instinct and learned behaviors are different. Underline examples of each.

A **behavior** is anything an organism does. **Learned behaviors** are behaviors that come from watching other animals or through experience. Young animals learn how to behave by watching and copying adults.

There are other behaviors. An **instinct** is a behavior that an animal knows without learning it. Animals are born with instincts. Behaviors are adaptations that may help an animal survive in its environment.

A mother lion teaches her cubs to hunt. Searching for food is an instinct. Knowing how to find and catch food is something cubs learn by copying their parents.

A mother sea turtle buries her eggs in the sand. Most young sea turtles hatch at night. Their instinct is to go toward the brightest area. This instinct helps the hatchlings find the ocean.

A chimpanzee isn't born knowing how to use a tool. It learns this behavior by watching others. Sometimes, a chimp may figure it out on its own.

It is an instinct for some birds to sing, but sometimes the songs they sing are learned from other birds.

A spider's web helps it survive. The web is sticky, so it traps insects. But how does a spider know how to spin a web? This is an instinctive behavior.

A moth's instinct is to use moonlight to find its way. That is why moths are attracted to porch lights.

► How are instincts and learned behaviors alike?

_____

_____

_____

_____

Finding Food

Hungry. Cold. Wet. That's what animals would be without the instinct to find food and shelter.

Active Reading As you read these two pages, underline details that tell ways animals find food. Circle ways animals find shelter.

Every animal looks for food when it's hungry. It's an instinctual behavior. But actually finding food can be a learned behavior. Some animals learn from watching their parents or other adults. But some animals can learn by themselves, too.

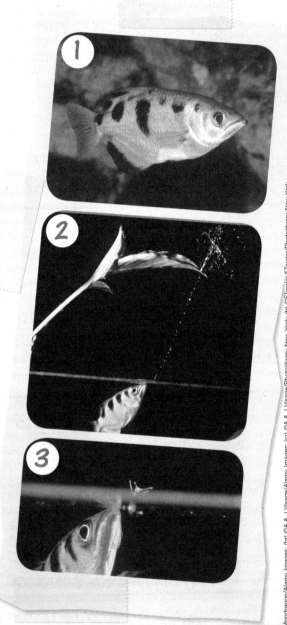

Bears come to this stream to catch salmon. The bears wait for the fish to swim upstream. This is a learned behavior.

How did this archerfish know how to get food from above the water? The fish instinctively shoots water at insects in the air to catch them.

Finding Shelter

These birds learned to build nests on buildings when trees were cut down.

A gopher uses what it has—soil and claws—to make a shelter in the ground.

How Animals Survive

How does building an anthill help the group of ants?

_____

_____

_____

_____

_____

_____

Ants work together to make an anthill. They use the soil around them. The hill hides a tunnel system that provides shelter and storage space for food.

Hibernation

When the weather turns cold, it is time for many animals to slow down.

Active Reading As you read these two pages, draw a line under the words that describe what is happening to the animals in the photos.

Animals respond to cold winter weather in different ways. Some animals stay active during winter. They find food or eat food they have hidden. Other animals **hibernate**, or go into a deep, sleeplike state that helps them survive the cold winter conditions. Normal body activities slow down. The heart beats slowly, and breathing almost stops. Hibernating is an instinctive behavior.

A hibernating animal doesn't use much energy, because its body is barely working. There is enough fat stored in the animal's body to keep it alive through the winter.

This ground squirrel spent the fall eating and gaining weight. It stored up enough energy to survive winter hibernation. The squirrel's heart rate and breathing have become slower.

Many bats like this one hibernate in the winter. In the spring when the weather warms up, there is more food for the bat. It will come out of hibernation.

Which animals hibernate? Many animals that eat insects hibernate. These animals include bats, hedgehogs, and hamsters. Insects such as ladybugs and bees also hibernate. So do lizards, snakes, turtles, skunks, badgers, and many more animals.

These snakes are all hibernating together. When spring arrives, they will leave this den.

Look at the Data

How does each animal's heart rate change during hibernation?

Animal's Heart Rate	Bat	Woodchuck
Non-hibernation	450 beats per minute	160 beats per minute
Hibernation	40 beats per minute	4 beats per minute

_____

_____

Migration

Some animals are travelers. Some whales make a yearly trip from someplace cold to someplace warm and back.

Active Reading As you read, compare the different reasons animals migrate. Circle each reason an animal might migrate.

Animals **migrate** when they move a long distance as a group from one region to another and back. Whales swim to a warm place to mate. They swim to a different spot to give birth. Then they swim back to where they were to find food.

Many animals, including birds and fish, migrate. Whales and some other animals teach their young the way to go. The path the animals take is learned, but knowing when to migrate is an instinct.

Gray whales have one of the longest migration routes of any mammal. They travel up to 21,000 kilometers each year. Gray whales swim from the cold Arctic to warm Mexico to have their young.

In the winter, when the land freezes over in the Arctic, tundra swans fly to the warmer south. When the weather warms up, the swans return to the Arctic. There, they mate and wait for their eggs to hatch.

Migration Routes of Gray Whales and Tundra Swans

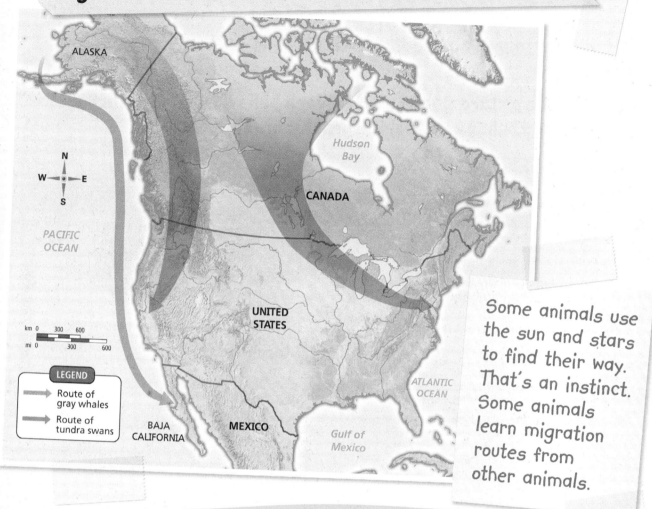

Some animals use the sun and stars to find their way. That's an instinct. Some animals learn migration routes from other animals.

Do the Math!
Make a Graph

Many animals migrate. The gray whale may travel over 10,000 kilometers each way as it migrates. The tundra swan may travel over 3,000 kilometers each way as it migrates. Draw a bar graph to compare the distances.

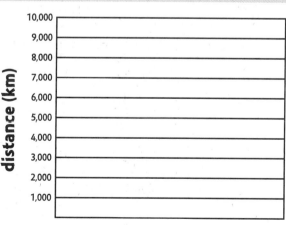

Sum It Up!

When you're done, use the answer key to check and revise your work.

Read the picture clues. Decide if each behavior is an instinct or a learned behavior. Label the graphic organizer.

1

Young sea turtles hatch and walk toward the ocean.

____

2

Chimps use tools like this stick to get food.

____

Behavioral Adaptations

3

Ground squirrels sleep through the winter when food is scarce.

____

4

Grizzly bears wait in the water to catch fish.

____

Answer Key: 1. instinct 2. learned behavior 3. instinct 4. learned behavior

© Houghton Mifflin Harcourt Publishing Company (bl) ©James Simon/Photo Researchers, Inc.; (br) ©Jeff Mondragon/Alamy Images; (tl) ©Mauricio Handler/Getty Images; (tr) ©WILDLIFE GmbH/Alamy Images

Brain Check

Name _____

Word Play

1 Use the words in the box to complete the puzzle.

adaptations	behavior*	instinct*	learn
migrate*	parent	shelter	hibernate*

*Key Lesson Vocabulary

Across

4. Behaviors are _____ that help organisms survive.

7. Animals that _____ enjoy a long winter's rest.

8. Animals _____ to hunt by watching other animals.

Down

1. A young animal learns behaviors by watching its _____.

2. Animals that need a warm place out of the rain seek _____.

3. Looking for food and shelter is an _____.

5. Each year, gray whales _____ thousands of miles.

6. Migration and hibernation are two examples of animal _____.

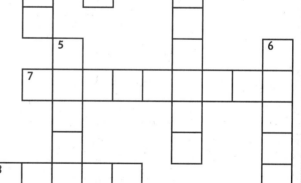

Apply Concepts

2 How are instincts and learned behaviors the same? What is the difference between them?

_____

_____

_____

3 Look at the photos. Construct an explanation about how the behavior helps the animal survive.

_____

_____

_____

_____

_____

_____

Take It Home!

Talk to your family about the things you do every day. Which things have you learned? Which are instincts?

Lesson **4**

Essential Question

What Are Ecosystems?

Engage Your Brain!

Find the answer to the following question in this lesson and record it here.

This woodpecker stores acorns in this tree. Why is the tree part of the woodpecker's habitat?

_____

_____

_____

Active Reading

Lesson Vocabulary

List the terms. As you learn about each one, make notes in the Interactive Glossary.

_____   _____

_____   _____

_____

Main Idea and Details

Detail sentences give information about a topic. The information may be examples, features, characteristics, or facts. Active readers stay focused on the topic when they ask, What fact or information does this sentence add to the topic?

Animals and Plants at Home

What do sand, salt water, crabs, and seaweed all have in common? You can find them at the beach, of course!

Active Reading As you read these two pages, draw two lines under each main idea.

When you go to the beach, you find lots of living things. Nonliving things, like sand and salt water, are also part of the beach. Everything that surrounds a living thing is its **environment**. This includes living and nonliving things. Your desk, teacher, books, and air are all part of your classroom environment.

An **ecosystem** is all of the living and nonliving things in a place. In an ecosystem, living things interact with each other and with the nonliving parts of their environment. Think of bees that use an old log to build their hive. They gather nectar from flowers to make honey. A bear eats the honey. These interactions make up a part of an ecosystem.

Living things in the same ecosystem share resources. Many of them also share a habitat. A **habitat** is the space where a plant or animal lives. A frog's habitat is a pond. A frog's environment is everything around the frog.

This crab's habitat is on the sand. The crab and sand are both part of an ecosystem.

232

An ocean ecosystem includes salt water, seaweed, fish, and other animals. Each depends upon the other to survive.

Sea anemones, sea stars, and mussels live in tide pools. They all share resources, such as food, to survive in their environment.

What Makes Up an Ecosystem?

Choose an ecosystem from the photographs. List at least three things that make up the ecosystem.

_____

_____

Communities of Populations

You live in a community. You are also part of a population. Animals and plants are part of populations in communities, too.

Active Reading As you read these two pages, find and underline an example of a population.

Wolves, bears, snakes, birds, and many other plants and animals all live in Yellowstone National Park. A **population** is all of one kind of organism living in the same area. All of the wolves in Yellowstone National Park make up a wolf population.

Animal and plant populations in an area may be a part of the same community. A **community** is all of the populations that live and interact in an area. An ecosystem can have many different communities.

Grassland Ecosystem

Yellowstone National Park has a large population of bison. The bison are part of a community that includes the grasses that bison eat and this population of antelope.

This bull snake is also part of the Yellowstone National Park community along with the wolves and bison.

This wolf is a part of the wolf population that lives in the same area. To survive, wolves eat other animals in their community.

Do the Math!
Make a Bar Graph

Use the data in the table to create a bar graph to compare populations of animals in a community within Yellowstone National Park.

Animal	Population
Bald Eagle	5
Gray Wolf	35
Elk	70
Bull Snake	15

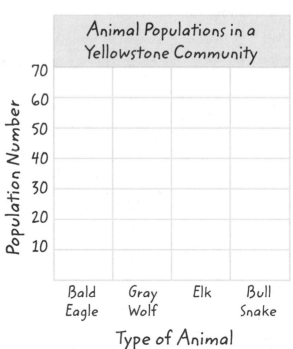

Animal Populations in a Yellowstone Community

Population Number

70
60
50
40
30
20
10

Bald Eagle · Gray Wolf · Elk · Bull Snake

Type of Animal

Living on the Land

You've seen that bison live in grassland ecosystems. What other types of land ecosystems are there?

Active Reading As you read these two pages, draw circles around the names of ecosystems that are described.

Forest ecosystems have a lot of trees. Tropical rain forests have many different kinds of trees. These forests are warm and wet all year long. Animals like jaguars, toucans, and monkeys live in tropical forests.

Some forests have warm summers and cold winters. Woodpeckers, squirrels, deer, and bears are common. The trees, such as oaks and maples, lose their leaves in the fall.

Other land ecosystems are shown on these two pages.

Desert Ecosystem

Kangaroo rats, rattlesnakes, and cactus populations live in deserts. They have adaptations that help them survive in this dry ecosystem.

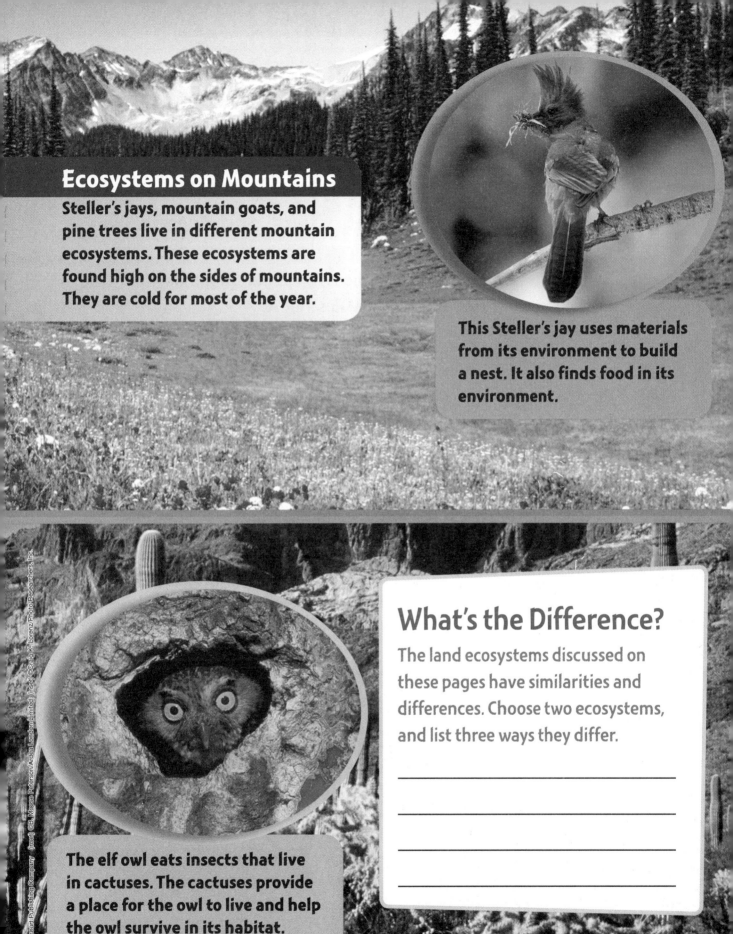

Ecosystems on Mountains

Steller's jays, mountain goats, and pine trees live in different mountain ecosystems. These ecosystems are found high on the sides of mountains. They are cold for most of the year.

This Steller's jay uses materials from its environment to build a nest. It also finds food in its environment.

What's the Difference?

The land ecosystems discussed on these pages have similarities and differences. Choose two ecosystems, and list three ways they differ.

_____

_____

_____

_____

The elf owl eats insects that live in cactuses. The cactuses provide a place for the owl to live and help the owl survive in its habitat.

Under the Water

Most of Earth is covered with water. There are many different living things below the surface of ponds, lakes, rivers, and oceans.

Active Reading As you read these two pages, draw a line from the picture to the sentences that describe it.

If you look at a globe, you'll notice a lot of blue! That blue represents Earth's oceans. The oceans consist of salt water. Animals like sea turtles, whales, and lobsters live in ocean ecosystems. Some ocean animals, like coral, don't look like animals at all. The ocean also has plantlike life forms such as kelp and seaweed.

Rivers, lakes, ponds, and streams are usually fresh water. Fresh water has much less salt than ocean water. Frogs, ducks, and many kinds of fish live in fresh water. Alligators are found in freshwater wetlands. Land animals like deer, foxes, and raccoons drink this fresh water.

Ocean Ecosystem

This huge underwater ecosystem is made by tiny ocean animals called corals.

Clownfish live around sea anemones in their habitat. The clownfish are immune to the anemone's stings, but animals that might eat the clownfish are not!

© Houghton Mifflin Harcourt Publishing Company   (b) ©Image Source/Getty Images; (t) ©Corbis; (inset) ©Digital Vision/Getty Images††

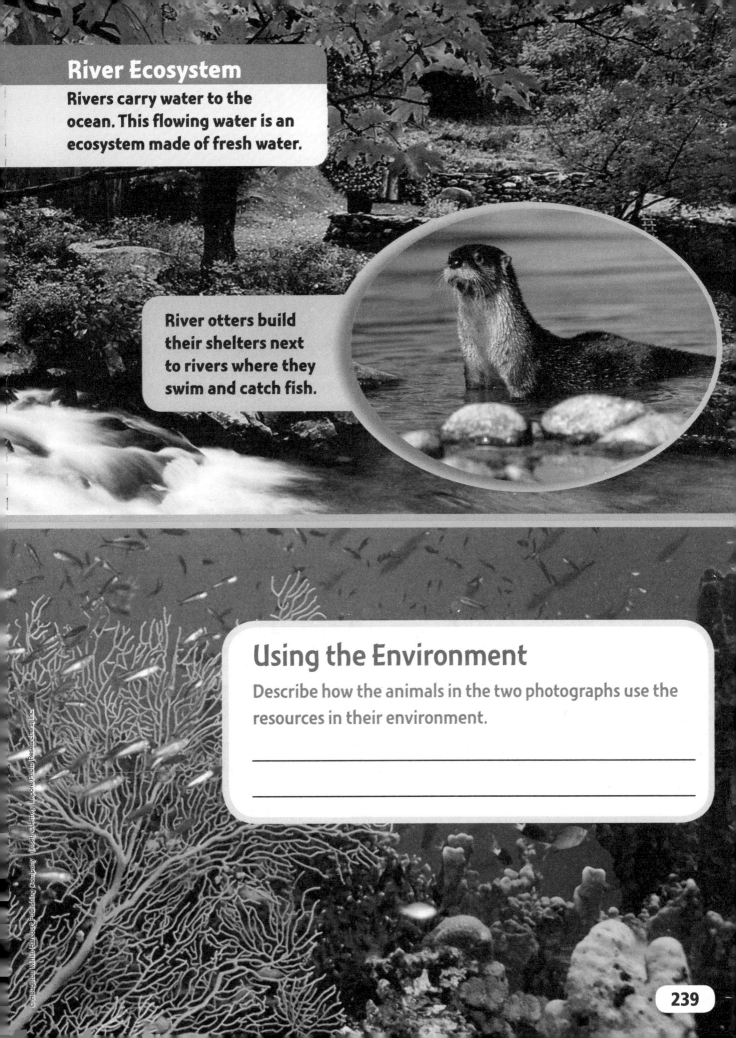

River Ecosystem

Rivers carry water to the ocean. This flowing water is an ecosystem made of fresh water.

River otters build their shelters next to rivers where they swim and catch fish.

Using the Environment

Describe how the animals in the two photographs use the resources in their environment.

_____

_____

Sum It Up!

When you're done, use the answer key to check
and revise your work.

**Read each statement. Draw a line to match each statement
with the picture it describes.**

1 This saltwater ecosystem covers much of the earth's surface.

Desert

2 This ecosystem's main plant is grass.

Ocean

3 This ecosystem has the cactus, a plant that stores water in its stem.

River

4 Steller's jays and mountain goats live in this ecosystem.

Mountain

5 Fox and deer drink the fresh water from this water ecosystem.

Grassland

240

Answer Key: 1–Ocean 2–Grassland 3–Desert 4–Mountain 5–River

Name _____

Word Play

1 Use the clues to help unscramble each word. Write the unscrambled word in the boxes.

1. NOACE
   This ecosystem contains salt water.
   ⬜⬜⬜⬜⬜

2. SLSADNAGR
   Bison and antelope roam this flat ecosystem.
   ⬜⬜⬜⬜⬜⬜⬜⬜⬜

3. SMCEYOTSE
   The living and nonliving things that interact in the same area.
   ⬜⬜⬜⬜⬜⬜⬜⬜⬜

4. TBHTAAI
   Where a plant or an animal lives.
   ⬜⬜⬜⬜⬜⬜⬜

5. NDPO
   Cattails and water lilies live near or on this freshwater ecosystem.
   ⬜⬜⬜⬜

6. TMVEINNRONE
   The living and nonliving things that surround a living thing.
   ⬜⬜⬜⬜⬜⬜⬜⬜⬜⬜⬜

7. YOMCNTUMI
   The populations that live in one place.
   ⬜⬜⬜⬜⬜⬜⬜⬜⬜

8. RTSEDE
   Plants and animals that can survive with little water live in this ecosystem.
   ⬜⬜⬜⬜⬜⬜

9. OLTOPNPUAI
   All of one type of organism in the same place.
   ⬜⬜⬜⬜⬜⬜⬜⬜⬜⬜

10. SATRORFENI
    Jaguars, toucans, and monkeys live in this ecosystem.
    ⬜⬜⬜⬜⬜⬜⬜⬜⬜⬜

Apply Concepts

2 In what kind of ecosystem would you find these living things? Write the name of the area underneath each one.

Clownfish

_____

Alligator

_____

Fish

_____

Zebra

_____

Cactus

_____

Toucan

_____

3 Choose an organism. Use evidence to construct an explanation of why the organism survives in its habitat and not in a different habitat.

_____

_____

_____

_____

_____

Take It Home!

See *ScienceSaurus*® for more information about ecosystems.

S3L1.a Georgia Plants, Animals, and Habitats; **S3L2.a** Effects of Pollution;
S3L2.b Protecting Plants and Animals

Lesson **5**

Essential Question

What Are Some Georgia Plants and Animals and How Can We Protect Them?

Engage Your Brain!

Find the answer to the following question in this lesson and record it here.

Where in Georgia do black bears live, and how can we protect them?

_____

_____

_____

Active Reading

Lesson Vocabulary
List the terms. As you read, make notes about them in the Interactive Glossary.

_____ _____

_____ _____

Compare and Contrast
Many ideas in this lesson show comparisons and contrasts—how things are alike and how things are different. Active readers stay focused by asking themselves, How are these things alike? How are these things different?

Blue Ridge Mountains

The land that makes up Georgia is classified into five areas called **geographic regions**. Two of them are the Blue Ridge Mountains and the Piedmont. What plants and animals are found in these regions?

Forests cover most of the Blue Ridge Mountain region.

Active Reading As you read, draw one line under names of plants and animals found in the Blue Ridge Mountains. Draw two lines under names of plants and animals that are found in the Piedmont.

The Blue Ridge Mountain region is covered mostly with forests. The region has deep valleys with steep sides called canyons. It also has many lakes, rivers, and waterfalls.

This region is cooler and wetter than many of Georgia's other regions. Winters are cold and summers are mild. Some areas can receive over 80 inches of rain each year!

Plants that grow in this region include oak trees, hickory trees, magnolia trees, shrubs, and grasses.

Animals include black bears, bobcats, deer, beavers, warblers, wild turkeys, salamanders, and trout. Animals that live in the higher mountains must be able to survive cold temperatures and windy conditions.

Many kinds of animals like this warbler live in the Blue Ridge Mountain region.

Piedmont

The Piedmont region in Georgia is south of the Blue Ridge Mountain region. It is made of low rolling hills and flat areas of land with few trees. Lakes, slow-moving rivers, and waterfalls are found throughout the region.

Winters are cool and summers are hot. The region receives about 50 inches of rain each year.

Oak trees, hickory trees, pine trees, dogwood trees, and wildflowers are some of the plants that grow in the Piedmont region.

Animals include opossums, river otters, beavers, deer, raccoons, owls, hawks, and eagles.

Many kinds of trees and other plants grow in the Piedmont region.

Raccoons are one kind of animal that lives in the Piedmont region. They hunt for food at night.

▶ How is the Blue Ridge Mountain region similar to the Piedmont region? How is it different?

Similar	Different

245

Coastal Plains

The Coastal Plains and the Valley and Ridge are two other geographical regions of Georgia. How can these regions be described?

Active Reading As you read, draw one line under the names of plants and animals that are found in the Coastal Plains region. Draw two lines under the names of plants and animals found in the Valley and Ridge region.

The Coastal Plains region is the largest habitat region in Georgia. The land is close to the ocean and is wide and flat. Wet habitats like marshes and swamps are part of this region.

It does not get very cold here. Winters are mild and summers are hot.

Plants that grow in the Coastal Plains region include oak trees, cypress trees, saw palmettos, and water lilies.

Animals include alligators, ducks, seagulls, snakes, lizards, turtles, frogs, crabs, clams, oysters, fish, and deer. Manatees swim to the coastal area of Georgia in the summer months.

Cypress trees grow in the wet areas of the Coastal Plains region.

Many alligators live in the swamps and marshes of Georgia's Coastal Plains region.

Valley and Ridge

The Valley and Ridge region is in the northwest area of Georgia. It is made of long, rocky mountains called ridges that are separated by lower areas called valleys. Forests cover a lot of the land. Rivers and natural hot springs are also found in this region.

Like many parts of Georgia, winters are cool and summers are warm. Temperatures can sometimes get below freezing in the winter. The region receives about 60 inches of rain each year.

Pine trees, oak trees, and grasses are some of the plants that grow in the Valley and Ridge region.

Animals of the Valley and Ridge region include crayfish, frogs, turtles, snakes, many kinds of fish, hawks, cardinals, deer, skunks, and opossums.

Reptiles like this turtle are able to stay warm enough in the Valley and Ridge region.

Which Is It?

Decide whether each plant or animal is usually found in the Coastal Plains or the Valley and Ridge region. Put a check mark in the correct column.

	Coastal Plains	Valley and Ridge
Crayfish		
Cypress tree		
Oyster		
Pine tree		

The Valley and Ridge region is made of flat valleys and taller ridges.

Appalachian Plateau

The Appalachian Plateau is the fifth geographical region of Georgia. How is it similar to the other regions? How is it different?

Active Reading As you read, draw a line under the plants and animals found in the Appalachian Plateau region.

The Appalachian Plateau is in the northwestern tip of Georgia. It is a plateau region. It is mostly flat land that rises above valleys and low-lying areas.

Temperatures here are similar to the Blue Ridge Mountain region. Winters are cold and summers are mild to hot and humid.

There are many forests. Plants include pine trees, hickory trees, tulip trees, oak trees, and mountain laurel.

Animals include black bears, foxes, bobcats, opossums, bats, grouse, hawks, salamanders, turtles, lizards, and snakes.

Asking Questions

Write three questions you can now answer about Georgia's geographical regions.

_____
_____
_____
_____

Effects of Pollution on Georgia's Plants and Animals

Wow! Did you know that what you do each day can affect Georgia's plants and animals in different ways?

Active Reading As you read, draw a box around the sentences that give key information about the main idea.

Simple actions such as riding in a car can harm the environment. Buses, cars, and trucks put pollution into the air. **Pollution** is any substance in the environment that can harm living things. Pollution can harm human health.

Pollution also comes from factories that burn coal for energy. The pollution can go into the air, into the soil, and into the water. It can harm living things and make the water less clean.

People build roads and houses. They cut down trees to make products from wood and to clear space. These actions destroy habitats in Georgia and all over the world. As a result, there is less living space for other living things.

Oil can spill from ships and pollute water. The oil can cover living things like seagulls. The animals must be cleaned, or they could get very sick.

Cars, trucks, and buses put pollution into the air.

249

Do the Math!
Interpret a Table

The table below shows how the number of cars in the United States has changed over time. Study the table, and then answer the questions.

1935	1956	2005
27 million	65 million	240 million

1. Between 1935 and 1956, the number of cars increased by how much?

_____

_____

2. Between 1956 and 2005, the number of cars increased by how much?

_____

_____

3. How might the increase in cars affect the environment?

_____

_____

_____

Boats move through rivers and oceans near manatees. Manatees swim slowly and can't always get out of the way when a boat is near. Sometimes they get struck by boats.

A landfill is a place where garbage is buried. If a landfill is not built properly, harmful chemicals from garbage get into soil and water.

Protecting Georgia's Plants and Animals

You can make a difference and help protect Georgia's plants and animals!

People can help protect Georgia's plants and animals by protecting their habitats. People can conserve natural resources. **Conservation** means using natural resources wisely.

We can plant new trees to replace trees that are cut down. People can plant gardens on rooftops. Rooftops, streets, and sidewalks take in and give off heat. Planting gardens on rooftops and trees in parks helps keep cities cool. Less air-conditioning is used and energy resources are saved.

People can also **recycle**, reuse, and reduce. Recycling means making something new from something used. Old soda cans are recycled into new cans.

Planting trees makes new habitats for living things. It also helps keep the soil in place.

How Can You Use It?

Suppose you have an old T-shirt. In the lines below, list some ways you can reuse the T-shirt. Try to come up with as many uses as possible. Share your list with the class.

_____

_____

_____

People can ride a bike or walk to nearby places. These actions reduce air pollution.

Sum It Up!

When you're done, use the answer key to check
and revise your work.

Write the name of the geographical region below each picture.

1 _____

4 _____

2 _____

5 _____

3 _____

Answer Key: 1. Appalachian Plateau 2. Blue Ridge Mountain 3. Coastal Plains 4. Piedmont 5. Valley and Ridge

Name _____

Word Play

1 Fill in the missing letters in each word. You will use each of the letters in the box.

> T C Y U I
> R A N V O

1. P ___ L L ___ T ___ O N
2. ___ E C ___ C L I N G
3. ___ O ___ S E R ___ A T I O N
4. H A B I ___ ___ T

Fill in the blanks with the correct words from above.

5. It is important to protect each _____ in Georgia's geographic regions.

6. Factories that burn coal can release _____ that harms the environment.

7. Using a plastic water bottle to make a bird feeder is an example of _____.

8. Using as little water as possible when taking a shower is an example of _____.

Apply Concepts

2 The chart shows some harmful actions of people on the environment. Next to each harmful action, write a helpful action that people can do to help the environment and protect the habitats of Georgia's plants and animals.

Harmful action	Helpful action
Cut down trees.	
Drive a car.	

3 Where in Georgia will you most likely find these living things? Write the name of the geographical region below each plant or animal.

alligator

dogwood tree

_____

_____

4 Pick two geographical regions of Georgia. Describe one way they are the same. Describe one way they are different.

_____

_____

_____

Take It Home! Write two questions you have about conservation efforts in Georgia. With a family member, do some research to find the answers to these questions.

Vocabulary Review

Use the terms in the box to complete the sentences.

> adaptation
> behavior
> ecosystem
> geographic region
> population

1. All of the same kind of organism living in one area is a(n) _____.

2. A bird building a nest is an example of a(n) _____.

3. An area of Earth that can be described by its characteristics is called a(n) _____.

4. All of the living and nonliving things in a place is a(n) _____.

5. The quill of a porcupine is a structural _____.

Science Concepts

Fill in the letter of the choice that best answers the question.

6. Animals live in a certain habitat depending on their traits and how they live. Look at the picture below. In which habitat do you think this animal lives?

Ⓐ a desert

Ⓑ a grassland

Ⓒ a rainforest

Ⓓ a river

7. A scientist studies a group of ducks that all live together in the same area. She records information about when they migrate. What part of an ecosystem is the scientist studying?

Ⓐ community

Ⓑ environment

Ⓒ habitat

Ⓓ population

Science Concepts

Fill in the letter of the choice that best answers the question.

8. Animals have many behaviors. Some are learned and some come from instinct. Which of the following behaviors is based on instinct?

   Ⓐ a chimpanzee using a tool to dig up insects

   Ⓑ bats hibernating in the winter months

   Ⓒ lion cubs imitating hunting behaviors of their mother

   Ⓓ a dog responding to its owner's commands

9. Oscar enjoys bird watching. His favorite bird is a warbler, but he can see them only during the month of September. After that, the warblers head south in search of food. What is the warbler's behavior an example of?

   Ⓐ camouflage

   Ⓑ hibernation

   Ⓒ migration

   Ⓓ mimicry

10. Which adaptation helps the gray fox to escape from predators?

    Ⓐ It has thick fur.

    Ⓑ It reproduces in the spring.

    Ⓒ It goes through hibernation.

    Ⓓ It has the ability to climb trees.

11. Animals have body structures that help them to find food and shelter or defend themselves from predators. Look at the picture below.

    What adaptation helps the cheetah compete with other animals for food?

    Ⓐ climbing ability

    Ⓑ a long life cycle

    Ⓒ fur to maintain body heat

    Ⓓ strong legs for high-speed hunting

12. Flowers come in many shapes, sizes, and colors. How is this a plant adaptation?

    Ⓐ The different flowers help make a garden look attractive.

    Ⓑ The different flowers help the plant get the most sunlight.

    Ⓒ The different flower types help the plant survive in different climates.

    Ⓓ The different flower types attract different kinds of insects to pollinate them.

13. Tanisha collects information about one of Georgia's geographical regions. She records the information below.

Plants Observed	Animals Observed
cypress trees, saw palmettos	seagulls, ducks, crabs

Tanisha is most likely collecting information from which region?

(A) Piedmont

(B) Coastal Plains

(C) Appalachian Plateau

(D) Blue Ridge Mountains

14. Shante is starting an environmental club at her school. Which activity is a direct way that students can reduce air pollution?

(A) carpool with friends or walk to school

(B) recycle cans and bottles

(C) leave lights on during the day

(D) use plastic bags instead of paper bags

15. A scientist is studying the behavior of chipmunks. She records the information below.

Month	Average Body Temperature (°F)
January	55
April	90
June	99
October	95

Which adaptation is shown in the table?

(A) camouflage   (C) migration

(B) hibernation   (D) mimicry

16. Which part of a cactus allows it to survive long periods of dry weather?

(A) It has very shallow roots.

(B) It has large, colorful flowers.

(C) It has thick stems to hold extra water.

(D) It has thin, sharp needles.

17. The male snowy owl is almost completely white. It lives near the Arctic Circle, where this adaptation helps it stay hidden while hunting. What type of adaptation is this?

(A) camouflage   (C) instinct

(B) hibernation   (D) mimicry

Apply Inquiry and Review the Big Idea

Write the answers to these questions.

18. David is investigating the ecosystem in his backyard. The picture shows his house and yard.

What are the living and nonliving parts of this ecosystem?

a. living

_____

b. nonliving

_____

Which parts of the picture would be part of a community?

_____

_____

19. Katerina is doing a project on adaptations in birds for the science fair. Explain how she could use the materials shown here as models to show how different birds are adapted to eating different foods.

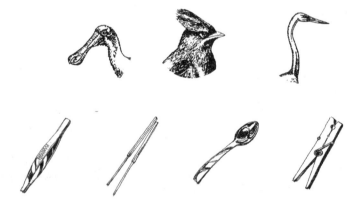

_____

_____

_____

21st Century Skills
Technology and Coding

Computer technology is all around us. You can use a desktop computer to study math, listen to music, or keep in touch with family. Many other devices, such as cell phones and digital cameras and camcorders, contain computer technology, too. How does this technology work? What problems can it solve? If you are interested in these questions, you might like computer science. *Computer science* is the study of computer technology.

Active Reading

As you read, underline examples of tools and devices that use computer technology.

Computers at work...

The word *compute* means to *do math*. Computers are devices that do math and perform tasks. For this reason, they are useful for many purposes. Biologists can use computers to record and analyze data about wildlife. Artists can use computers to model lifelike animations. Computer scientists study and develop computer technology. They might use their knowledge to improve existing devices or to create new ones.

What are some ways that you use computers?

_____

_____

_____

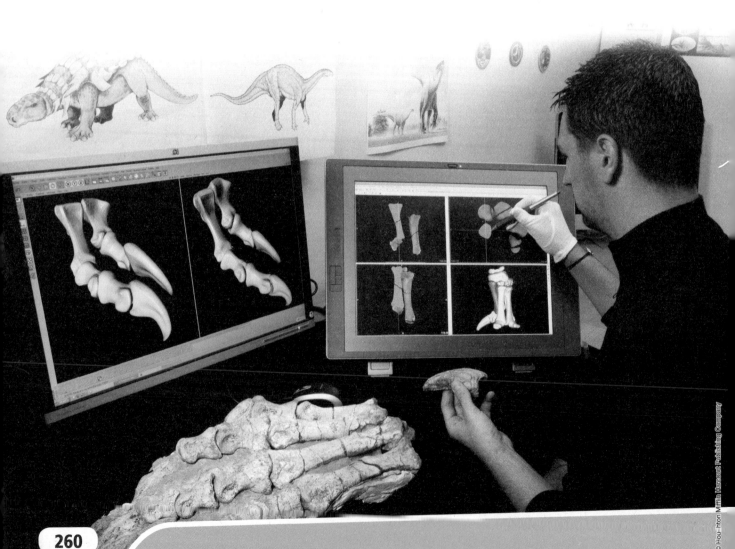

Many fields, such as medicine and education, rely on some kind of computer technology. Computer scientists can apply their skills to many different tasks. Working in computer science is a bit like solving a puzzle. Computer scientists think logically and creatively to solve problems. They often collaborate with others.

The students pictured here are using computer technology to build something fun: a robotic vehicle!

Let's talk

Computers carry out tasks by following instructions, or *programs*, that people design. Examples of computer programs include websites, mobile games, and digital photo editors. Computer programs are sometimes called *software*, *applications*, or *apps*.

Computer programs are not written in human language. They are written in a special programming language, or *code*, that the computer can interpret. If you learn how to write code, you can write computer programs, too!

```
15
16  # Check if player has grown 5 tomatoes and 5 carrots
17  if tomato_count >= 5 and carrot_count >= 5:
18      print ("Congratulations! Get ready for Round 2.")
19  else:
        print ("Keep working on your garden.")
```

If you want to work with computers, you need to learn to speak their language

Computer programs must be carefully planned.
Let's take a look at an example.

Imagine you want to create a video game about taking care
of a garden. You want to allow the player to provide water,
shade, and plant food. As you design your game, you must
think of all the actions the player could take. How should the
game respond if plants get too much water? Or not enough
sunlight?

Complete the cause-and-effect chart to plan how your gardening
program should respond to different player actions.

IF player overwaters garden → THEN plants turn yellow

IF player uses plant food → THEN _____

IF _____ → THEN _____

IF _____ → THEN _____

Take care

Always use computers safely and responsibly.

- ✓ Handle computers and other electronic devices carefully. They can be damaged if dropped.

- ✓ Protect electronic devices from dust, dirt, and moisture.

- ✓ Electric current can be dangerous. Tell an adult if you see damaged device cables or exposed wires.

- ✓ Do not share private information such as your phone number, address, or passwords.

- ✓ Talk to your family about rules for Internet use.

- ✓ Limit the time you spend on electronic devices. Take frequent breaks to exercise or stretch.

In the space provided, create a poster advertising computer safety tips.

Read the following statements and circle the best response.

You see a damaged power cable on a printer.

- Tell an adult
- Remove the cable and try to repair it

Someone you don't know wants to trade photos online.

- Send photos
- Ignore the request

Your homework requires more online reading than usual.

- Take breaks
- Do the entire assignment all at once

Careers in Computing

Medical professionals often use computer programs that are made especially for their work. For example, many veterinarians use special veterinary programs that store animals' health records and appointment schedules. These custom systems are designed by software developers. Software developers plan, create, and test computer programs. They consider the needs of users and collect feedback to improve their programs. Software developers must have good communication and problem-solving skills.

Interactive Glossary

As you learn about each term, add notes, drawings, or sentences in the extra space. This will help you remember what the terms mean. Here are some examples.

Fungi [FUHN•jeye] A kingdom of organisms that have a nucleus and get nutrients by decomposing other organisms

A mushroom is from the kingdom Fungi.

physical change [FIHZ•ih•kuhl CHAYNJ] Change in the size, shape, or state of matter with no new substance being formed

When I cut paper, the paper has a physical change.

Glossary Pronunciation Key

With every glossary term, there is also a phonetic respelling. A phonetic respelling writes the word the way it sounds, which can help you pronounce new or unfamiliar words. Use this key to help you understand the respellings.

Sound	As in	Phonetic Respelling	Sound	As in	Phonetic Respelling
a	bat	(BAT)	oh	over	(OH•ver)
ah	lock	(LAHK)	oo	pool	(POOL)
air	rare	(RAIR)	ow	out	(OWT)
ar	argue	(AR•gyoo)	oy	foil	(FOYL)
aw	law	(LAW)	s	cell	(SEL)
ay	face	(FAYS)		sit	(SIT)
ch	chapel	(CHAP•uhl)	sh	sheep	(SHEEP)
e	test	(TEST)	th	that	(THAT)
	metric	(MEH•trik)		thin	(THIN)
ee	eat	(EET)	u	pull	(PUL)
	feet	(FEET)	uh	medal	(MED•uhl)
	ski	(SKEE)		talent	(TAL•uhnt)
er	paper	(PAY•per)		pencil	(PEN•suhl)
	fern	(FERN)		onion	(UHN•yuhn)
eye	idea	(eye•DEE•uh)		playful	(PLAY•fuhl)
i	bit	(BIT)		dull	(DUHL)
ing	going	(GOH•ing)	y	yes	(YES)
k	card	(KARD)		ripe	(RYP)
	kite	(KYT)	z	bags	(BAGZ)
ngk	bank	(BANGK)	zh	treasure	(TREZH•er)

Interactive Glossary

A

absorb [uhb•ZORB] To take in (p. 187)

adaptation [ad•uhp•TAY•shuhn] A trait or characteristic that helps an organism survive (p. 204)

amber [AM•buhr] Fossilized tree sap (p. 143)

B

bar graph [BAHR GRAF] A graph using parallel bars of varying lengths to show comparison (p. 37)

behavior [bih•HAYV•yer] The way an organism usually acts in a certain situation (p. 220)

C

camouflage [KAM•uh•flazh] The coloring, marking, or other physical appearance of an organism that helps it blend in with its surroundings (p. 208)

chart [CHART] A display that organizes data into rows and columns (p. 37)

clay [KLAY] The smallest particles of rock that make up soil (p. 110)

community [kuh•MYOO•nih•tee] All the populations of organisms that live and interact in an area (p. 234)

design process [dih•ZYN PRAHS•es] The process of applying basic principles of engineering to solve problems (p. 56)

conservation [kahn•ser•VAY•shuhn] Using natural resources wisely (p. 251)

E

ecosystem [EE•koh•sis•tuhm] A community of organisms and the physical environment in which they live (p. 232)

D

data [DAY•tuh] Individual facts, statistics, and items of information (p. 35)

environment [en•VY•ruhn•muhnt] All the living and nonliving things that surround and affect an organism (p. 232)

data table [DAY•tuh TAY•buhl] A kind of chart used for recording number data (p. 37)

erosion [uh•ROH•zhuhn] The process of moving weathered rock and soil from one place to another (p. 124)

Interactive Glossary

evidence [EV•uh•duhns] Data collected during an investigation (p. 35)

glacier [GLAY•sher] A large, thick sheet of slow-moving ice (p. 124)

experiment [ek•SPAIR•uh•muhnt] A test done to see whether a hypothesis is correct (p. 11)

graduated cylinder [GRAJ•oo•ay•tid SIL•in•der] A container marked with a graded scale used for measuring liquids (p. 21)

F

fossil [FAHS•uhl] The remains or traces of a plant or an animal that lived long ago (p. 143)

H

habitat [HAB•ih•tat] The place where an organism lives and can find everything it needs to survive (p. 232)

G

geographic region [jee•oh•GRAF•ihk REE•juhn] An area of Earth that can be described by its characteristics (p. 244)

heat [HEET] Energy that moves from warmer to cooler objects (p. 168)

© Houghton Mifflin Harcourt Publishing Company

hibernate [HY•ber•nayt] To go into a deep, sleeplike state for winter (p. 224)

instinct [IN•stinkt] An inherited behavior of an animal that helps it meet its needs (p. 220)

humus [HYOO•muhs] The remains of decayed plants or animals in the soil (p. 106)

investigation [in•ves•tuh•GAY•shuhn] A procedure carried out to carefully observe, study, or test something in order to learn more about it (p. 9)

hypothesis [hy•PAHTH•uh•sis] A possible answer to a question that can be tested to see if it is correct (p. 10)

L

learned behavior [LERND bee•HAYV•yer] A behavior that an animal doesn't begin life with but develops as a result of experience or by observing other animals (p. 220)

I

infer [in•FER] To draw a conclusion about something (p. 6)

M

map [MAP] A picture that shows the locations of things (p. 37)

Interactive Glossary

microscope [MY•kruh•skohp] A tool that makes an object look several times bigger than it is (p. 19)

model [MOD•l] A representation of something real that is too big, too small, or that has too many parts to be studied directly (p. 36)

migrate [MY•grayt] To travel from one place to another and back again (p. 226)

N

nutrients [NOO•tree•uhnts] Substances in soil that plants need to grow and stay healthy (p. 112)

mimicry [MIHM•ih•kree] An adaptation in which a harmless animal looks like an animal that is poisonous or that tastes bad, so that predators avoid it (p. 208)

O

observe [uhb•ZURV] To use your senses to gather information (p. 6)

mineral [MIN•er•uhl] A nonliving solid that has a crystal form (p. 92)

P

paleontologist [pay•lee•uhn•TAHL•uh•jist] A scientist who studies fossils (p. 148) pollution [puh•LOO•shuhn] Any substance in the environment that can harm living things (p. 249)

reflect [ri•FLEKT] To bounce off (p. 187)

population [pahp•yuh•LAY•shuhn] All the organisms of the same kind that live together in an ecosystem (p. 234)

S

sand [SAND] The largest particles of rock that make up soil (p. 110)

predict [pri•DIKT] To use observations and data to form an idea of what will happen under certain conditions (p. 8)

silt [SILT] Particles of rock that are smaller than sand but larger than clay (p. 110)

R

recycle [ree•SYE•kuhl] To make something new from something that has been used before (p. 251)

soil [SOYL] A mixture of water, air, tiny pieces of rock, and humus (p. 106)

Interactive Glossary

T

technology [tek•NOL•uh•jee] Anything that people make or do that changes the natural world (p. 70)

temperature [TEM•per•uh•cher] A measure of how hot or cold something is (pp. 23, 169)

V

variable [VAIR•ee•uh•buhl] The one thing that changes in an experiment (p. 11)

W

weathering [WETH•er•ing] The breaking down of rocks on Earth's surface into smaller pieces (p. 122)

Index

Index

© Houghton Mifflin Harcourt Publishing Company

Index

Index